"Follow Me."
The Invitation in Mark

"Follow Me."
The Invitation in Mark

LARRY S. McKAUGHAN

WIPF & STOCK · Eugene, Oregon

"FOLLOW ME." THE INVITATION IN MARK.

Copyright © 2019 Larry S. McKaughan. All rights reserved. Except for brief quotations in critical publications or reviews, no part of this book may be reproduced in any manner without prior written permission from the publisher. Write: Permissions, Wipf and Stock Publishers, 199 W. 8th Ave., Suite 3, Eugene, OR 97401.

Wipf & Stock
An Imprint of Wipf and Stock Publishers
199 W. 8th Ave., Suite 3
Eugene, OR 97401

www.wipfandstock.com

PAPERBACK ISBN: 978-1-5326-7512-6
HARDCOVER ISBN: 978-1-5326-7513-3
EBOOK ISBN: 978-1-5326-7514-0

Manufactured in the U.S.A.   JUNE 11, 2019

The text of the Gospel of Mark and most Scripture quotations are taken from The New Revised Standard Version of the Bible, copyright © 1989 National Council of the Churches of Christ in the United States of America. Used by permission. All rights reserved worldwide. (NRSV)

The Songs of the Servant of Yahweh and occasional additional verses are taken from The Jerusalem Bible, copyright © 1966 by Darton, Longman & Todd, Ltd., and Doubleday, a division of Penguin Random House LLC. Reprinted by permission. All rights reserved worldwide. (JB)

Occasional verses are quoted from the Revised Standard Version of the Bible, copyright © 1952 National Council of the Churches of Christ in the United States of America. Used by permission. All rights reserved worldwide. (RSV)

Occasional verses are quoted from the Authorized (King James) Version. Rights in the Authorized Version in the United Kingdom are vested in the Crown. Reproduced by permission of the Crown's pantentee, Cambridge University Press. (KJV)

This book is dedicated to my wife
Nancy Jane Gordon McKaughan

and to our children
James Larry McKaughan *in memorium*
Lara Sue McKaughan Boles
Daniel Jon McKaughan

Contents

Acknowledgment / ix

Introduction / xi

Mark Chapter 1 / 1

Mark Chapter 2 / 14

Mark Chapter 3 / 22

Mark Chapter 4 / 29

Mark Chapter 5 / 41

Mark Chapter 6 / 47

Mark Chapter 7 / 54

Mark Chapter 8 / 60

Mark Chapter 9 / 70

Mark Chapter 10 / 79

Mark Chapter 11 / 89

Mark Chapter 12 / 98

Mark Chapter 13 / 106

Mark Chapter 14 / 115

Mark Chapter 15 / 130

Mark Chapter 16 / 138

Postscript / 141

Songs of the Servant of Yahweh / 144

Bibliography / 155

Acknowledgment

I THANK DAN MCKAUGHAN for reading and offering comments on the book.

Introduction

MARK IS THE EARLIEST Gospel written. It is short. It moves quickly. The Gospel is written in *koiné* Greek, the rough language spoken by commoners and not the polished Greek of literature.

The title, "According to Mark," was not put there by the author. Others affixed it to the book at the time the four Gospels were made part of the Christian canon several centuries later. In a tradition of the early church that is cautiously accepted by many contemporary scholars, the author was the John Mark spoken of in the book of Acts. The earliest recorded comment about Mark outside of the New Testament was attributed to Papias by the church historian Eusebius. Papias was bishop of Hierapolis, a city of Asia Minor, in the early decades of the second century.

Papias stated that "Mark, having become the interpreter/translator of Peter, wrote down accurately, however, not in order, all that he recalled of what was either said or done by the Lord. For he had neither heard nor followed the Lord; but later (as I said) he followed Peter. . . . Mark did no wrong in thus writing down some things as he recalled them, for he made it his aim to omit nothing he had heard and to state nothing therein falsely."[1]

In this tradition, then, John Mark was not one of the original followers of Jesus but listened to the disciple Peter tell his stories about Jesus and wrote those stories down. Papias believed that Mark's record accurately reflected Peter's account.

Mark probably finished his Gospel some time before the fall of Jerusalem to the Romans in 70 CE. Matthew and Luke later incorporated much of Mark's structure and most of his text into their own accounts of Jesus' life. The Gospel of John tells the story of Jesus from its own distinct vantage.

---

1. Eusebius, *Ecclesiastical History* 3.39.15–16. This translation is found in Brown, *Introduction to the New Testament*, 158.

Introduction

Mark's unpolished stories present a man of great goodness and power who was able to confront persons with the truth about who we are, yet beckon us to him with an empowering vision of the persons we can become.

The word "gospel," which means "good news," is particularly appropriate for the book of Mark. Of the four Gospel authors Mark alone applies this word to his own text (1:1) and Jesus calls the message he brings "good news" numerous times in Mark (1:14, 15; 8:35; 10:29; 13:10; 14:9).

Mark narrates a series of episodes in which Jesus teaches, acts forcefully, and is repeatedly challenged. Mark's Jesus brings to life some of the great biblical themes: the kingdom of God, a perspective on the character of the Messiah, and the bold invitation, "Follow me." Yet Mark refuses to provide the reader with easy answers. Why do the first disciples suddenly drop everything they have been doing to follow Jesus? Mark does not tell us. Mark's treatment of faith seems tangibly human. The disciples follow Jesus long before they are ready to claim that he is the Messiah. And when they reach that point, the belief they come to is apparently the wrong understanding of the Messiah. The disciples repeatedly stumble and fall short as soon as we get them into focus, and Mark never lets up. He does not try to explain Jesus' acts of power or the resurrection. Why, for instance, does Mark leave us abruptly at the empty tomb in the original ending of the book (16:8)? His lack of easy answers is combined with a subtlety and irony that can speak powerfully to modern readers.

The present study began as a seminar for young adults. It is written for inquirers, for persons who don't mind raising questions, who want to read the Gospel of Mark intelligently and would like to know enough about the background setting to be able to understand the tensions represented in the give and take of participants in Mark's text.

I am particularly interested in the person of Jesus portrayed by Mark. My aim in the present study is to set out to understand Jesus in the text as Mark wrote it, avoiding as much as possible theological assumptions about Jesus that come from a later age, be it contemporary historical/critical, or from the Council of Nicea. Scholarly sources will be used, however, to help us understand first-century Judaism. We will pay particular attention to quotations Mark provides as context for the story he is presenting.

The boldface Mark text for this commentary (with one exception) and most other direct biblical quotations come from the *New Revised Standard Version* (NRSV) translation. The Songs of the Servant of Yahweh come from the *Jerusalem Bible* (JB) translation. Other Bible translations will be

Introduction

credited when they are used. The comment sections include paraphrased quotations and my own translations based on my study of Mark's Greek text.

If we simply study Mark as history or as literature we can miss the intense personal significance an encounter with Jesus can have. Jesus often addressed persons as individuals. I desire to be open to a first person response to Jesus and hope that readers will also be open to such a response. Thus this study is written not only in third person but sometimes finds expression in first and second person. Mark was an intelligent writer. What happens if we allow Mark's Jesus to teach us what it means to be a Christian?

On a personal note, I was tormented for a number of years over certain doctrines that I had been taught a Christian had to believe. Not that I necessarily believed them to be false; but I was not able to persuade myself that they were positively true and affirm them as my own. One day, after talking to a Presbyterian minister, I realized that if I had to believe that Jesus was God-man—I simply was not a Christian. While it was in some sense freeing to face that truth, it also tormented me. I began trying to figure out which doctrines would be absolutely essential to being a Christian. Somehow I was unable to get enough traction on that course to move on.

After graduate school in psychology I taught a liberal arts seminar one term at the University of Oregon entitled, "In Search of Stature." We explored characteristics that give stature, nobility, or courage, to Homer's Odysseus, Plato's Socrates, Abraham in Genesis, and Mark's Jesus, among others. I recall lying on the rug of our rented cottage in front of a Ben Franklin stove one morning to read the Gospel of Mark assignment. I opened the book to begin reading.

I met him there.

He was walking on the pebbly shore of the Sea of Galilee. He watched Simon Peter and his brother Andrew cast a net into the lake, for they were fishermen. Jesus said to them, "Follow me, and I will make you fishers of men." At once they left their nets and followed him.

The story shocked me in its vividness, its simplicity, in what was not said. Jesus did not walk down the beach with an arm over Peter's shoulder interrogating him. He did not ask, first thing, "Do you believe that I am God incarnate?" and double-check for accuracy. No. He said simply, "Follow me. I will teach you to make something more of your life."

At that moment I heard his voice, "Larry, *you* follow me."

"That," I answered emphatically, "is something I can do!"

Introduction

It was a moment of ecstasy for me. I felt a sudden weight lift. The shackles of creeds that had tormented me broke loose. I experienced the freedom of new insight for the way.

So I followed Jesus and with Peter, Andrew, and two other brothers, James and John, I followed him through the book of Mark. I discovered that in Mark and in the other Gospels, "Follow me" is a characteristic way Jesus has of inviting people along his path. Not the only way, of course. And I discovered that the meaning of the invitation to follow him takes on added depth somewhere along the line. But for starters you and I, and Matthew, and others, are invited to come and see.

Why study Mark? If we can share the chance to meet Jesus in his element, if we let Jesus define for us the astounding freedom that his invitation offers, if we learn from the powerful and demanding love his life embodies, we will discover what it means to follow him.

Mark Chapter 1

1 The beginning of the good news of Jesus Christ, the Son of God.

FROM VERSE 1, MARK sets out to provide a narrative of the good news embodied in Jesus' ministry. That it is a beginning may imply that Mark expects this narrative to have an importance beyond the confines of his text. The sense in which this story can be good news for us as well as the original audience is something each of us must explore as we engage with Mark's account. What Mark means in calling Jesus the Christ and the Son of God will be given substance even as Mark writes.

We should note that this first sentence sets up a form of irony for the entire book. It identifies Jesus for the reader and the listener in a way that goes beyond what we could possibly know if we were among the human participants in the story that unfolds. The words of Jesus might shock us, and some of his deeds would certainly amaze us as they happen before our eyes, but we would likely miss the irony in having, say, someone thought to be demon-crazed correctly identify Jesus long before the rest of us reached that conclusion.

> **2 As it is written in the prophet Isaiah,**
> **"See, I am sending my messenger ahead of you,**
> **who will prepare your way;**
> **3 the voice of one crying out in the wilderness:**
> **'Prepare the way of the Lord,**
> **make his paths straight.'"**

"Follow Me."

Mark immediately ties the first sentence of his book into Jewish Scripture with an explicit quote from the prophet Isaiah. So the good news that Mark begins to tell comes not as an isolated event but is to be understood in context of Jewish Scripture and tradition.

The voice crying in the wilderness quotes Isaiah 40:3. God calls his people, who in this Isaiah's time were exiles in Babylon, to come back quickly to Jerusalem through the wilderness to be comforted. Why? "Here is your God!" (40:9). The messenger who shouts this message is twice called the "herald of good tidings" in verse 9. Thus the context of Isaiah 40 clarifies for us who sends the messenger, and that the good news is that God's people are to come home.

The first part of Mark's quote, however, is not from Isaiah at all. "I am going to send an angel in front of you, to guard you on the way and to bring you to the place that I have prepared," comes from Exodus 23:20, in which God tells the Israelites they will be led into the promised land. (Note that the Hebrew word for "angel" can also be translated "messenger," as it is in the next quote.) In Malachi 3:1 we find the words, "See, I am sending my messenger to prepare the way before me, . . . the messenger of the covenant in whom you delight." Portions of both verses seem to be included in Mark's quote.

Mark has fused two or more passages in his quote from Scripture.[1] It was a common practice of rabbis in Mark's day to study Scripture by using words or phrases that several passages held in common. In fusing passages like this, a commentator can broaden or sharpen the application of the words quoted, and we in turn can learn what the commentator wants to emphasize. In each of the three verses Mark alludes to, God is addressing the people of God. The messenger sent ahead, the command to prepare the way of God, and a path through the wilderness will become motifs that echo through the book of Mark.

> **4 John the baptizer appeared in the wilderness, proclaiming a baptism of repentance for the forgiveness of sins. 5 And people from the whole Judean countryside and all the people of Jerusalem were going out to him, and were baptized by him in the river Jordan, confessing their sins. 6 Now John was clothed with camel's hair, with a leather belt around his waist, and he ate locusts and wild honey. 7**

---

1. Mark does this repeatedly. Markus, *Way of the Lord*, 15, which includes a list of fused references in Mark.

> **He proclaimed, "The one who is more powerful than I is coming after me; I am not worthy to stoop down and untie the thong of his sandals. 8 I have baptized you with water; but he will baptize you with the Holy Spirit."**

What is John's baptism? The phrase "repentance for the forgiveness of sins" is worth considering. "Repent"—*metanoeite* in Greek—has the characteristic Greek emphasis of "change your mind," or "pursue another purpose." Since John the Baptizer was a Jew who was probably speaking Hebrew or Aramaic, we should note that the Hebrew verb for repent, *shuvu*, means to turn around or to return, and was used repeatedly in Scripture to call God's people to abandon any idolatry, to give up selfish riches, to turn from injustice, and to live in God's presence.

One is to turn away from *hamartia*, which can mean a sinful life, or missing the mark, a mistake, an error in judgment, or a single sin. The act of turning away involves a change of heart that allows a person to be forgiven, set free from bondage, delivered, and pardoned.

Thus, John comes to the wilderness of the Jordan River preparing God's way. He preaches something like this, "Turn from your errors to a better path. God forgives a repentant sinner. Make your life a path worthy of God." God's cleansing forgiveness is then enacted when the person is baptized by John in the Jordan.

There were general precedents for baptism in John's time. Converts to Judaism were admitted to the faith in a ceremony that included baptism.[2] The convert turned from another path to the Jewish way of life. The sharp edge in John's preaching is that he cries out to Jews that they too need to repent and be baptized. The assuring welcome is that God forgives the repentant sinner.

Why do the crowds come into the wilderness to find John? Most Jews of Jesus' day believed that the present age (*ha'olam haze*) of suffering under Roman oppression would pass and be replaced by a time promised by the prophets when God restores his kingdom on earth, the age to come (*ha'olam haba*). It would be a time of peace, of justice, and of wealth enough for every family to own a fig tree and grape arbor; a time of respect from other nations who would come to Zion to worship their God. As Mark's account proceeds it seems likely that John's baptism of repentance was seen as preparation for that promise.

---

2. Flemington, "Baptism," 348. The men in the Qumran community also had a ritual bath to cleanse themselves before worship. Betz, "Dead Sea Scrolls," 798.

"Follow Me."

John the Baptist is designated a wilderness man a second time when attention is brought to his diet and garb, which in turn make allusion to Elijah the prophet who wore a hairy cloak with a leather belt around his waist (2 Kgs 1:7–8). But given the context of the above Isaiah verses, the hint that John the Baptist is identified with Elijah provides another allusion to the prophet Malachi, who said, "I will send you the prophet Elijah before the great and terrible day of the Lord comes" (Mal 4:5).

The cumulative impact of these allusions is that John is the messenger sent ahead to prepare the way. Mark immediately confirms this impression by quoting John the Baptist preaching that he will be followed by someone more powerful than himself, one who will baptize not with water but with God's Holy Spirit.

> **9 In those days Jesus came from Nazareth of Galilee and was baptized by John in the Jordan. 10 And just as he was coming up out of the water, he saw the heavens torn apart and the Spirit descending like a dove on him. 11 And a voice came from heaven, "You are my Son, the Beloved; with you I am well pleased."**

Mark immediately introduces us to the man who comes after John the Baptist. He is baptized. And we are given a confirmation of an important portion of the first sentence of the book. Jesus is called "beloved Son" and the path on which he is walking is affirmed by the voice from heaven.

The spirit with which Jesus will baptize others now descends on Jesus, the Holy Spirit of God. Mark uses a harsh, even violent word here, the passive voice of the Greek verb *schizo*, to be ripped, to be torn. The heavens are torn apart for the Spirit to descend.

Jesus is baptized in water by John with the common folk, a baptism of repentance. At that moment in the form of a dove the Spirit circles down. Jesus experiences a baptism by God's anointing. This makes Jesus an "anointed" one, which is "Messiah" in Hebrew, "Christ" in Greek. These events confirm another portion of Mark's first sentence.

The words the divine voice speaks allude to two verses, Psalm 2:7 and Isaiah 42:1. Psalm 2 is a messianic psalm. David was God's anointed king. In the psalm David speaks, saying: "The Lord [God] said to me, 'You are my son; today I have begotten you.'" In Isaiah 42:1 God says, "Here is my servant whom I uphold, my chosen, in whom my soul delights. I have put my spirit upon him."

The voice from heaven thus speaks as a father to a son. It affirms Jesus as Son, hinting at the lineage of king David; and Jesus, God's beloved, pleasing to God, is anointed with God's Spirit.

12 And the Spirit immediately drove him out into the wilderness. 13 He was in the wilderness forty days, tempted by Satan; and he was with the wild beasts; and the angels waited on him.

Mark states that the Spirit drove Jesus into the wilderness. We might expect that Jesus needs time to sort out the practical way in which he will pursue his task, if he is *the* expected Messiah of the Jews. He may be struggling with the profound tension that exists between the contexts of the two verses alluded to by the voice from heaven.

We should note in passing that many Jews of Jesus' day were expecting the Messiah, a hope based on God's promise to David relayed by the prophet Nathan: "I will raise up your offspring after you . . . and establish the throne of his kingdom forever. I will be a father to him, and he shall be a son to me. When he commits iniquity, I will punish him with a rod such as mortals use" (2 Sam 7:12–14). This prophecy is celebrated in many biblical texts. But as one king after another in David's line was unfaithful to God, the prophets called them to task, predicted punishment, even exile; and they began to project the promise to David into the future. Isaiah 11 develops the messianic theme, singing of a shoot that springs from the stock of Jesse (David's father). "The spirit of the Lord shall rest on him, the spirit of wisdom and understanding. . . . With righteousness he shall judge the poor and decide with equity for the meek of the earth. He shall strike the earth with the rod of his mouth and with the breath of his lips he shall kill the wicked" (Isa 11:1–2, 4).

The voice from heaven called Jesus "beloved son." Psalm 2 begins with God laughing at the kings of the earth who set themselves against the Lord God and his anointed. And immediately after calling the anointed king "son" in verse 7, God says: "Ask of me, and I will make the nations your heritage, and the ends of the earth your possession. You shall break them with a rod of iron, and dash them in pieces like a potter's vessel" (Ps 2:8–9). The image of a military king modeled on King David, one who conquers the nations that oppress the Jews, became a dominant component of the hoped-for Messiah. The Jewish scholar Geza Vermes finds that a study of "ancient Jewish prayer and Bible interpretation demonstrate

"Follow Me."

unequivocally" that the people of Jesus' day expected the Messiah to be "a person endowed with the combined talents of soldierly prowess, righteousness and holiness."[3] But the psalm certainly does not make clear just how the anointed one is to combine military qualities with the above mentioned wisdom and righteousness.

In contrast, the Isaiah passage alluded to by the voice expressing God's pleasure in Jesus was not even considered to be messianic. "Here is my servant, whom I uphold, my chosen, in whom my soul delights" (Isa 42:1 NRSV), is followed by the words: "I have put my spirit upon him; he will bring forth justice to the nations. He will not cry or lift up his voice, or make it heard in the street; a bruised reed he will not break, and a dimly burning wick he will not quench; he will faithfully bring forth justice. He will not grow faint or be crushed until he has established justice in the earth" (42:2–4). Thus begins the first of four songs that make explicit mention of the servant of God. Who is this servant? Sometimes called Israel, sometimes he is a person who is to save Israel; the servant will provide leadership that brings justice to all peoples of the earth. Over the course of these songs the portrait is pushed in the direction of the servant enduring explicit insult, injury, and death.[4] There is no hint of military action for this servant. But if this portrait were to become a model, just how would the servant bring justice to his people, let alone to all the earth?

Can these options—to rule with a kingly military force or to serve with a firm but gentle touch—even be reconciled with each other? Jesus is presented with making choices in the wilderness and finding a practical outcome such that his life can continue to echo the voice come from heaven.

Mark does not even characterize Satan for us in chapter 1 except to say that he tested Jesus. The verb used, *peirazo*, can mean to make proof of, to attempt, to test, or to tempt. Since the Spirit that has just descended on Jesus drives Jesus into the wilderness, perhaps Satan is cooperating with the Spirit by testing Jesus' character.[5] On the other hand, if the power of

---

3. This was the commonly expected Messiah of the Jews. Vermes, *Jesus the Jew*, 134. Other messianic hopes were not so widespread. The Qumran community expected three messianic figures: a priest (based on their reading of Deuteronomy 33:8–11), a king (based on Numbers 24:15–17), and a prophet like Moses (based on Deuteronomy 18:18–19). Vermes, *Jesus the Jew*, 137. The Samaritans hoped for a prophet like Moses.

4. God's servant is the focus in each of these songs. See the final section of the present book, "Songs of the Servant of Yahweh."

5. In Jewish Scripture, Satan is an accuser or prosecutor in God's court rather than

God has just broken through into the world at the baptism, Satan, who may represent the powers of this world, gets an immediate confrontation with the new power in Jesus.

We must wait for Mark's further characterization of Satan before drawing conclusions about how Satan tests Jesus. And we must study the remainder of the book of Mark to find how Jesus resolves the tension over his task. Mark tells us that Jesus was in the wilderness with wild animals for forty days. He states that angels (or messengers), apparently from God's side, waited on Jesus.

> **14 Now after John was arrested, Jesus came to Galilee, proclaiming the good news of God, 15 and saying, "The time is fulfilled, and the kingdom of God has come near; repent, and believe in the good news."**

Suddenly John the Baptist is moved from the scene. We learn later that he sits prisoner in the dungeon of Herod Antipas, the Jewish ruler of Galilee. Jesus moves from John's wilderness quarters to the greener, more populous Galilee. He takes up the theme of repentance and forgiveness where John left off but with a new emphasis on the kingdom of God.

"The kingdom of God is at hand," other translations put it. Many of his listeners must have heard the promised age to come in these words. But I am convinced that Jesus' focus is on the nearness of *God's* kingdom in a sense that opens the offer to us in our age as well. It is good news. Another portion of Mark's first sentence is confirmed.

Why does Jesus start out with "Repent!" so like John the Baptist? Turn around! Go in a different direction than the course you have chosen for yourself! Jesus even associates this with good news. What can be so good about the invitation to repent?

John the Baptist called people to a renewal of life, to walk in the way in which God wants us to walk. Jesus comes, and the kingdom of God breaks in with him. He tells us that God's realm is close by both in place and time. God's kingdom is near at hand. Now! Not just in chronological clock time (which would be *cronos*), but in *kairos*, the full measure of time, the ripe season. The opportune moment has arrived. Don't simply repent of your

---

a distinctive demonic figure who is opposed to God and responsible for all evil (See, for example, Job 1–2 or Zechariah 3:1–2). Satan began to emerge as a distinct evil opponent of God and humans in the intertestamental writings of the second and first centuries BCE. Gaster, "Satan," 224–28.

"Follow Me."

deeds. Believe in (*pisteuete*), have faith in, give credence to, trust the good news. The realm of God is within reach!

Jesus' invitation is not simply a call for a solitary act of repentance, trust, and reconciliation between each person and God. We are invited to join God's community, to live within God's realm rather than our own. That is the alternative, of course, to choosing our own rule to live by.

Can repentance be good? Can there be a better place for humans to begin than to stand in the presence of our Creator and honestly confess who we are, our sins, our mistakes, our limitations; to find that God's grace is generous enough to forgive us, to prepare us to become the persons we are meant to be in God's kingdom? It is humbling. It is ennobling.

This invitation embodies something essential in how Jesus so effectively relates to all kinds of people in sometimes desperate need: he heals the sick, he parties with reknowned sinners, he touches the leper outcast, and ministers to persons who have almost given up hope. He does not brandish our sins before the world. He meets us honestly on the point of human sin, yet meets us with the love of already knowing the work of God's willing forgiving and renewal, already seeing the higher way for our lives.

> **16 As Jesus passed along the Sea of Galilee, he saw Simon and his brother Andrew casting a net into the sea—for they were fishermen. 17 And Jesus said to them, "Follow me and I will make you fish for people." 18 And immediately they left their nets and followed him. 19 As he went a little farther, he saw James son of Zebedee and his brother John, who were in their boat mending the nets. 20 Immediately he called them; and they left their father Zebedee in the boat with the hired men, and followed him.**

Mark does not tell us whether Simon, Andrew, James, or John had ever seen or heard of this man beforehand. We can grant that Jesus' invitation is striking, but the words alone, "Follow me and I will make you fish for people," would not seem to be enough to compel a person to follow him. But if Jesus has been traveling around Galilee preaching what he calls the good news, the word likely gets around. They've heard of John the Baptist. Rumors may fly about the new man. Perhaps these fishermen have had a chance to hear him for themselves. Perhaps Jesus has seen them respond to him in a crowd. Mark does not tell.

Jesus finds them at work, casting nets into the Sea of Galilee. One kind of net fishermen used on the Sea of Galilee in those days and up to the present spreads out like a parachute when it is cast, weights tugging at the outer edges of the net with a drawstring through the middle of the chute which, pulled at the right instant, closes the net to encircle a fish or a school of fish. Galilee fishermen also used long nets with corks along the surface that can be stretched between boats.[6] When I fished for salmon in Alaska I discovered that people who fish with nets must spend hours mending their nets, like James and John, because strands of the net come untied or break when fish try to get through the mesh.

Jesus approaches them with a new invitation, not the call to repentance. He says, speaking in Aramaic or Hebrew, *leku acharai*, literally, "Walk after me." In the Greek it is *deute opiso mou*, "Come behind me." This invitation comes with a promise. "Follow me, and I will make you into fishers of men," as *The Jerusalem Bible* translates it. The Greek word *anthropon* used here is the generic "men," which means humans. The invitation is to become fishers of women, children, and men.

What about this promise to Simon and Andrew, and perhaps to James and John that first day, to "make you fishers of men"? I find the translation "fishers of" preferable to the NRSV "fish for" because it speaks in vocational terms rather than of simple acts. Jesus touches the trade in which these men find themselves employed and uses that as a metaphor for something more that he invites them to become. Instead of fish, the focus of the new way of life will involve a concern for humans. The invitation makes strong contact with the work they are doing. Perhaps they are to fish with a new purpose, or leave their boats behind forever. Just what might Jesus mean? They follow him to find out.

This invitation is *so Jesus*, so characteristic of the way Jesus meets you at a practical point in your everyday life and calls you to follow him. In context of the good news Jesus proclaims in Galilee, is it not an invitation to explore what it means to walk in God's kingdom? Well, come and see.

21 They went to Capernaum; and when the sabbath came, he entered the synagogue and taught. 22 They were astounded at his teaching, for he taught them as one having authority, and not as the scribes.

Jesus came from the wilderness to the shores of Galilee. Now he enters a synagogue in nearby Capernaum with four men to join a gathering of Jews for worship. Invited to speak, he teaches and his teaching makes quite

---

6. Wolf, "Fishing," 273–74.

"Follow Me."

an impression (Mark 1:22, 27). Mark does not tell us what Jesus taught in Capernaum. We might expect that his message is a variation on what he has said before, "Believe that God's kingdom is near. Repent. God welcomes you."

Among the listeners are scribes. Scribes are an elite group of men trained in the Jewish Scriptures, the educated leaders in the synagogues, the interpreters of the Law of Moses. An ordained scribe can be a judge in criminal and civil cases.[7] A synagogue of people normally defers to their scribes as their rabbis.

The scribes will want to know with what authority Jesus speaks, what verses of Scripture justify his claims, how is God's kingdom closer than before, and how can sinners be welcome in God's kingdom? These are appropriate questions to ask, no more than a part of the ongoing dialogue that every educated Jew has with the community and with the Scripture. Jesus evidently responds with ease. The Capernaum participants see their scribes put on the defensive, and the scribes find themselves on the short end of their congregation's comparison with Jesus' teaching and authority.

> **23 Just then there was in their synagogue a man with an unclean spirit, 24 and he cried out, "What have you to do with us, Jesus of Nazareth? Have you come to destroy us? I know who you are, the Holy One of God." 25 But Jesus rebuked him, saying, "Be silent, and come out of him!" 26 And the unclean spirit, convulsing him and crying out with a loud voice, came out of him. 27 They were all amazed, and they kept on asking one another, "What is this? A new teaching—with authority! He commands even the unclean spirits, and they obey him." 28 At once his fame began to spread throughout the surrounding region of Galilee.**

This gathering is startled when a man suddenly cries out, "I know who you are, Jesus of Nazareth, the Holy One of God!" and adds the ominous question, "Have you come to destroy us?" All of this happens so quickly. The man is characterized as someone possessed by an unclean spirit, and he gives his answer to the scribes' question about authority, in a way that confirms Mark's initial characterization of Jesus. Jesus commands him to be silent and commands the unclean spirit to leave this man. There are convulsions, a loud cry, and then silence. We are not told what Jesus does next. Does he lean over to help him up? Does he embrace the man as a brother?

---

7. Jeremias, *Jerusalem in the Time of Jesus*, 234–37, 243, 253–54.

Others in the gathering simply cannot stay quiet. What is this? A new teaching! And with authority over unclean spirits!

> **29 As soon as they left the synagogue, they entered the house of Simon and Andrew, with James and John. 30 Now Simon's mother-in-law was in bed with a fever, and they told him about her at once. 31 He came and took her by the hand and lifted her up. Then the fever left her, and she began to serve them.**

Jesus goes with the four who are following him to a nearby house. There he meets Simon's mother-in-law and responds to her immediate need. Jesus will often speak with the person he ministers to, extend his hand to touch the individual, and the person is healed. It seems that this particular healing, like the synagogue exorcism, takes place before sundown, the official end of Sabbath. It foreshadows a controversy over Jesus doing unnecessary healing during the Sabbath. What will these acts teach us about Jesus' values on the relative importance of keeping the letter of the Law of Moses and, say, ministering to individual humans?

Simon's mother-in-law, for her part, jumps up and immediately ministers to Jesus and those who are with him. The verb used is *diakoneo*, to serve or minister to, a word Christians would later appropriate for the title "deacon." She throws herself into a serving work.

> **32 That evening, at sundown, they brought to him all who were sick or possessed with demons. 33 And the whole city was gathered around the door. 34 And he cured many who were sick with various diseases, and cast out many demons; and he would not permit the demons to speak, because they knew him.**

As soon as Sabbath was over it seems like all Capernaum gathers at Simon's door. Jesus heals many that night. He silences the demon-possessed. Mark emphasizes their ironic recognition of Jesus. But why does Jesus silence them? Why keep it secret? Why not proclaim that he is the Messiah from the start?

> **35 In the morning, while it was still very dark, he got up and went out to a deserted place, and there he prayed. 36 And Simon and his companions hunted for him. 37 When they found him, they said to him, "Everyone is searching for you." 38 He answered, "Let us go on to the neighboring**

> towns, so that I may proclaim the message there also; for that is what I came out to do." 39 And he went throughout Galilee, proclaiming the message in their synagogues and casting out demons.

Jesus retreats from the crowds to be alone. He centers himself in prayer with God, his Father in heaven, perhaps to lift up his day, to replenish his spirit, to find direction for further work. This act suggests a continuing of the relationship we first witnessed at Jesus' baptism. When those who followed him found him, Jesus was focused on his task: to keep proclaiming his message of repentance and of God's kingdom in the villages of Galilee.

Simon is featured among the disciples in chapter 1 of Mark. Mark's narrative of the morning search, Jesus' healing of Simon's mother-in-law in his own home, and Jesus' personal invitation to follow him, all relate stories Simon Peter would have told in first person. He is mentioned more frequently than any other disciple in the Gospel of Mark.[8] This is no proof, of course, that Peter was the main source for Mark's narrative. But it reminds us that it is a narrative about individual lives and the impact Jesus had on many.

> **40 A leper came to him begging him, and kneeling he said to him, "If you choose, you can make me clean." 41 Moved with pity, Jesus stretched out his hand and touched him, and said to him, "I do choose. Be made clean!" 42 Immediately the leprosy left him, and he was made clean. 43 After sternly warning him he sent him away at once, 44 saying to him, "See that you say nothing to anyone; but go, show yourself to the priest, and offer for your cleansing what Moses commanded, as a testimony to them." 45 But he went out and began to proclaim it freely, and to spread the word, so that Jesus could no longer go into a town openly, but stayed out in the country; and people came to him from every quarter.**

In the Jewish purity code anyone who touched a person with leprosy or another skin disease was defiled, made unclean, and would have to undergo

---

8. Jesus names Simon "Peter" when he names the apostles in 3:16–19. He is referred to as Simon or Peter 25 times in Mark. James is mentioned 11 times (5 times with Peter), John 10 times (5 times with Peter), Andrew 4 times (3 times with his brother). Judas Iscariot is named 3 times. The other seven disciples are mentioned once each except for Matthew who is called Levi in Mark 2:14 and 15.

a purification ritual. As a result of this ruling, lepers often lived in their own village outside the walls of a town and would cry out, "Unclean! Unclean," when walking along the way lest even their shadow touch another person. On this occasion the effects of the purity code were reversed. Jesus reaches out, touches this leper, and makes him whole, clean.

Mark Chapter 2

2 When he returned to Capernaum after some days, it was reported that he was at home. 2 So many gathered around that there was no longer room for them, not even in front of the door; and he was speaking the word to them. 3 Then some people came, bringing to him a paralyzed man, carried by four of them. 4 And when they could not bring him to Jesus because of the crowd, they removed the roof above him; and after having dug through it, they let down the mat on which the paralytic lay.

WHILE THE CROWDS GATHER to listen to Jesus and to watch him, we get the wonderful details of the episode of the paralytic youth borne by four companions on a mat. From the street they enter an inner courtyard that serves this group of dwellings. They try to get through the mob but there is no way to get close to the door of the house where Jesus is speaking. The four use outdoor stairs from the inner court to get the young man to the roof. There they dig through the dried earth mixture, pull out branches, and make a hole large enough to lower their friend on his mat to the hands reaching up from below.

An archeological dig in Capernaum (Tell Hum) has found a dwelling under what was an octagonal Byzantine church a short distance south of the old synagogue. The first-century dwelling is judged to be a commoner's house because there was no mortar in its unhewn basalt rock walls. Such walls could not support an upper class masonry roof or vault. They would, however, have supported the beams, tree branches, and a mixture of earth and straw that made up the roof of a commoner's house. Christian graffiti and prayers using the names of Jesus and Peter were found on plaster remnants from the old dwelling level, as well as coins dating from Agrippa's rule. Archeologists wonder, might this have been Peter's house? It seems to have been a Jewish Christian house church for a time and the Byzantine church with mortar in its walls was built on top of that.[1] Jesus was standing in such a house.

Those standing with Jesus are getting dusted. Dry mud falls in their eyes and twigs fall all around. In the commotion the people push back against the crowd to make room. They reach up. They lower the young man to the floor in front of Jesus.

> **5 When Jesus saw their faith, he said to the paralytic, "Son, your sins are forgiven." 6 Now some of the scribes were sitting there, questioning in their hearts. 7 "Why does this fellow speak in this way? It is blasphemy! Who can forgive sins but God alone?" 8 At once Jesus perceived in his spirit that they were discussing these questions among themselves; and he said to them, "Why do you raise such questions in your hearts? 9 Which is easier, to say to the paralytic, 'Your sins are forgiven,' or to say, 'Stand up and take your mat and walk'? 10 But so that you may know that the Son of Man has authority on earth to forgive sins"—he said to the paralytic— 11 "I say to you, stand up, take your mat and go to your home." 12 And he stood up, and immediately took the mat and went out before all of them; so that they were all amazed and glorified God, saying, "We have never seen anything like this!"**

The scribes have not openly accused Jesus of blasphemy here. The scribes, as we have seen, are the guardians of tradition and interpreters of the Law. It is their responsibility to judge the appropriateness of any action. They must, out of a personal and professional commitment, deal with what Jesus has just said and done. Jesus also understands the issues involved here. When he sees the scribes look around and whisper among themselves, he knows they wonder, *Who does this man from Nazareth think he is? He welcomes sinners into God's kingdom. Now he thinks he can forgive sins. But God alone can forgive sins!*

---

1. Corbo, *House of St. Peter at Capharnaum*, 37. The house excavated at Tell Hum is part of just such a complex of "clan" dwellings around a court as described in the previous paragraph.

"Follow Me."

The passive, "Your sins are forgiven," should probably be read as "God forgives your sins." In saying this, however, Jesus is at least claiming the right to speak on God's behalf here. But Jesus goes on to make the stronger claim that he, who calls himself the Son of Man, has authority to forgive sins on earth, and that includes this paralytic's sins.

Blasphemy implies an irreverence toward God. An arrogant defiance of God would be blasphemous. One can blaspheme God's spirit, God's name, God's will. The Jews know God as one who forgives sin (e.g., Exod 34:6–7; Ps 130:3–4). Is Jesus arrogantly taking for himself God's role as the divine forgiver, and then using his power to heal as proof that he has authority to forgive sins on earth? Jesus knows such an act may be judged blasphemous. But consider alternatively: is Jesus trying to make it clear that the power of God in his kingdom has come, is indeed present, and that sins are forgiven, that trust in God can make a person whole in body as well as in spirit?

This is the first time Jesus refers to himself as "the Son of Man." In the book of Ezekiel, God constantly addressed the prophet as "Son of man" when he commanded him to prophesy and to write down his visions.[2] Probably more important is the fact that the title "son of man" appears in Daniel 7:13 (JB), a verse Jesus will later use in claiming to be the Messiah. In Daniel's vision "one like a son of man" appears before God, the Ancient of Days, and is given dominion over all the nations and all the people on earth. Jesus gives the name a definite article and uses *the* Son of Man as a self-designating title rather than call himself a prophet or the Messiah. He asserts here that "the Son of Man has *authority* on earth to forgive sins," a startling, perhaps alarming, claim to make.

> **13 Jesus went out again beside the sea; the whole crowd gathered around him, and he taught them. 14 As he was walking along, he saw Levi son of Alpheus sitting at the tax booth, and he said to him, "Follow me." And he got up and followed him.**

Capernaum was a town on the northwest edge of the Sea of Galilee close to the border with Perea, a territory on the other side of the Jordan River. Tolls were collected in tax booths along the road. The toll collectors were usually Jews employed by Jewish kings such as Herod or by Roman administrators. They had a widespread reputation for dishonesty. Often skimming the taxes

---

2. "Son of man" is used 93 times in Ezekiel, e.g., Ezekiel 2:1 (JB).

collected, they represented the oppressive political order and they were a class shunned by the Jews. Yet Jesus invites Levi to follow him; in the presence of many who would despise Levi, given the crowd that has gathered, Jesus invites him to become a disciple.

> **15 And as he sat at dinner in Levi's house, many tax collectors and sinners were also sitting with Jesus and his disciples—for there were many who followed him. 16 When the scribes of the Pharisees saw that he was eating with sinners and tax collectors, they said to his disciples, "Why does he eat with tax collectors and sinners?" 17 When Jesus heard this, he said to them, "Those who are well have no need of a physician, but those who are sick; I have come to call not the righteous but sinners."**

It seems that Levi is so happy to be invited to follow Jesus that he throws a party for him. Jews sat up straight for ordinary meals but reclined on the left elbow for festive meals. The verb *katakeimai* is used here. Jesus reclined at Levi's party surrounded by his disciples with a sizable group of non-observant Jews and disreputable folk who also follow Jesus.

Note the precision of Mark's designation of the group to raise this question when they see Jesus eating and drinking with such a motley group of sinners. These are scribes associated with the Pharisee faction of the priesthood. To put this group in their first-century context requires a brief digression.

In Jesus' time the chief priests and elders, a priestly and lay nobility, made up one faction of the priesthood called the Sadducees. The Sadducees advocated cooperating with the Romans. Rome and Herod appointed the high priest. The Sadducees maintained their position of power by forging an accommodation with the foreign rulers. They had become a conservative aristocracy among the Jews with a strong power base in Jerusalem. The Torah spelled out laws for personal purity and laws pertaining to food that were to be honored by the priests. The Sadducees held that these priestly purity laws were strictly limited to the priests and their families, in conformity with a literal reading of the Scripture.

The Pharisees, on the other hand, were found in synagogues throughout the land; these were priests who pursued a vision calling the entire nation to be a holy people. The Pharisees took the verse of Leviticus 19:2, "You shall be holy, for I the Lord your God am holy," and insisted that these words and the priestly purity laws apply to all God's people. They began an

"FOLLOW ME."

oral tradition interpreting the Law of Moses in practical situations, "building a fence around the law" to help commoners keep from breaking the law. Many of the Pharisees were not trained as scribes but they all carefully observed this purity code and taught others to do so as well. Their hope was that when all the people observed the purity code, *that* day, the kingdom of God would come.

A third group of priests, the Essenes, believed they could observe the Law of Moses rigorously only by withdrawing from the mainstream of society with their families. Both the Pharisees and the Essenes opposed an accommodation with the Romans. The Qumran Essenes set up their community in the wilderness to prepare the way of the Lord.

A natural problem, given the strict demands of the purity code, was that many Jews were not fully observant of the code. People were categorized by how observant they were. This depended on personal behavior, physical purity, and to some extent who they were by birth. Priests and Levites ranked highest among the "righteous." The chronically ill, the maimed, and lepers ranked low among "sinners" and "outcasts." Tax collectors were just about off the list.[3]

Jesus has preached from the start that the kingdom of God is open to repentant sinners. In his actions Jesus has refused to make the purity code the supreme value of his life. He has touched lepers to heal them. He has invited common fishermen and tax collectors to follow him, and joins in parties with such folk!

The Pharisees were interested in seeing that food purity laws and regulations covering table fellowship be widely observed. You should be careful with whom you eat because table fellowship implies an acceptance of the other person, who that person is, and what that person does. And it is the scribes of the Pharisees who ask why Jesus is eating a fine meal in the company of tax collectors and sinners.

We are witnessing here an intense conflict between Jewish leaders who share many values in common. Jesus and the Pharisees are committed to bringing God's kingdom home. They agree that God's call to be holy applies to all the people. The scribes of the Pharisees respect Jesus enough to honor him with questions that challenge his approach. They engage with him in the living dialogue of Jew with Jew concerning the practice of God's Law in all aspects of one's daily life. But Jesus justifies his action in a way that shows

---

3. Jeremias, *Jerusalem in the Time of Jesus*, 271–74, 303–12. For the Pharisees see 246–47, 251–54, 263–67, for Sadducees 228–31, and Essenes 247, 259–61.

that he is consciously willing to contradict, and he knows that his actions may even undermine, the purity code as practiced by his questioners. He gives eating with sinners a higher priority than practicing a righteousness code that excludes them, and he makes calling sinners a central purpose in his life.

> 18 Now John's disciples and the Pharisees were fasting; and people came and said to him, "Why do John's disciples and the disciples of the Pharisees fast, but your disciples do not fast?" 19 Jesus said to them, "The wedding guests cannot fast while the bridegroom is with them, can they? As long as they have the bridegroom with them they cannot fast. 20 The days will come when the bridegroom is taken away from them, and they will fast on that day."

John the Baptist was more austere than the Pharisees, dressing simply, living in the wilderness. Jesus, by contrast, surprises us. He enjoys wine. He and his disciples do not even fast during the standard time for religious fasting. Why not? We must thank the friends of some annoyed disciple who asked the question.

Jesus' answer is a surprise. You don't fast at a wedding celebration. This, the present, is a time for rejoicing. And his answer implies that he has a special role in this party analogous to that of a bridegroom. He, his person, is the answer. The one who bears good tidings is present. As long as he is present his disciples will not fast.

Think how this answer rubs the disciples of the Pharisees. Jesus continues his answer with two metaphors that can apply to this entire series of interactions with the Pharisees.

> 21 "No one sews a piece of unshrunk cloth on an old cloak; otherwise, the patch pulls away from it, the new from the old, and a worse tear is made. 22 And no one puts new wine into old wineskins; otherwise, the wine will burst the skins, and the wine is lost and so are the skins; but one puts new wine into fresh wineskins."

The saying about sewing a new patch on old cloth is straightforward. The second saying works if we realize that wine was stored in fresh goatskins that stretched as the wine fermented. New wine will burst old wineskins.

But what do these metaphors allude to? What is this new wine? What is this new cloth? Jesus speaks here in context of a set of questions raised about various practices: the people with whom one eats and associates, and fasting, an exercise of devotion in relationship to God. Taken within the larger context of the kingdom of God that Jesus is ushering in, the claim is that there is something new here, something more valuable than rigidly following the religious expectations and purity codes that are commonly practiced. What is happening now, with himself present, Jesus claims, is more important than fasting. But we must travel further with Jesus to fill out details, to more fully taste this new wine and discover its aroma.

> **23 One sabbath he was going through the grainfields; and as they made their way his disciples began to pluck heads of grain. 24 The Pharisees said to him, "Look, why are they doing what is not lawful on the sabbath?" 25 And he said to them, "Have you never read what David did when he and his companions were hungry and in need of food? 26 He entered the house of God, when Abiathar was high priest, and ate the bread of the Presence, which is not lawful for any but the priests to eat, and he gave some to his companions." 27 Then he said to them, "The sabbath was made for humankind, and not humankind for the sabbath; 28 so the Son of Man is lord even of the sabbath."**

Deuteronomy 23:25 explicitly allows plucking your neighbor's standing grain if you are in need, but you may not put a sickle to it. What is at issue here is not that the disciples are plucking grain but that they are doing work on the Sabbath. The Pharisees sometimes debated just how many grains could be plucked before it constituted work that would defile this day set aside for rest.

Jesus defends his disciples by citing not the oral tradition of the Pharisees but an incident mentioned in 1 Samuel 21:1–6. David was fleeing the fury of King Saul. David asked the high priest for bread. The only bread available was the holy Bread of the Presence set apart and dedicated to God, which David took—five loaves, for he was hungry.

What kind of an answer is that? If David broke the Law of Moses, then Jesus and his disciples can break the Law because of hunger? Of course, at that point in the story David had secretly been anointed king but he had not yet become king. Does this answer suggest that a secretly anointed Son of David and his disciples should be allowed to break the Law if they are hungry? Is that the excuse?

The claim that "The sabbath was made for man, not man for the sabbath" (JB) expresses an opinion similar to one associated with the disciples of Hillel, an important Jewish teacher who lived in the generation before Jesus. This judgment is thus well within the reach of Jewish debate exploring the underlying purpose of and human obligations on the Sabbath.

But the next claim reaches radically farther. This is the second time Jesus has used the phrase "Son of Man" as a self referent in Mark. (We miss some linguistic connections in these verses by translating *anthropon* as the explicitly inclusive "humankind" rather than "man" in 2:27 because the "Son of Man" in 2:28 is also Son of *anthropon*.) Jesus claims to be lord even of the Sabbath!

What this claim amounts to is unclear, particularly when we look at it from a frame of reference like that of the Pharisees. Is Jesus claiming merely that hungry humans are more important than Sabbath laws? He puts it too provocatively to mean only that. Is Jesus asserting that the Messiah has a right to break the Sabbath laws, to break the purity code, and that he is the Messiah? But why would God's Messiah want to break the law that God handed to his people through Moses? Is Jesus saying that the Pharisees have made the law more rigid than God intended it, so that they use the law to enslave people rather than free them? The Sabbath was meant as a day of rest to remind people that they are free, that they are God's people, that God is to be served. We should keep the Sabbath and not break it!

The simplest solution may be the one suggested by the first line in the book of Mark. God's Christ *is* given authority to forgive sins on earth and has authority to interpret the Law of Moses so as to express God's intention in giving the law. This solution has to be the least acceptable interpretation to the Pharisees. If every Jew starts following the example of this man, some Pharisees would argue, the Law of Moses will be undermined and the kingdom of God will never come to us!

Must the kingdom of God bring such friction upon us? Was that first unclean spirit right when it cried out, asking, "Have you come to destroy us?"

Mark Chapter 3

> 3 Again he entered the synagogue, and a man was there who had a withered hand. 2 They watched him to see whether he would cure him on the sabbath, so that they might accuse him. 3 And he said to the man who had the withered hand, "Come forward." 4 Then he said to them, "Is it lawful to do good or to do harm on the sabbath, to save life or to kill?" But they were silent. 5 He looked around at them with anger; he was grieved at their hardness of heart and said to the man, "Stretch out your hand." He stretched it out, and his hand was restored. 6 The Pharisees went out and immediately conspired with the Herodians against him, how to destroy him.

YOU EXPECT HIS OPPONENTS to set up a test to challenge Jesus, particularly after Jesus' claim to be lord over the Sabbath. The conflict between the Pharisees and Jesus, which has been intensifying since the end of chapter 1, begins to come to a head. Jesus enters the Capernaum synagogue. Jesus may even be a little late. Already present are the Pharisees, some men from Herod's palace (with whom Pharisees are not usually friendly), a man with a withered hand, and others of the congregation. Jesus appreciates the fact that a problem is presented to him. He decides to handle it as part of his ongoing dialogue about how God wants us to use the Sabbath. Jesus calls the man forward and asks his question, "Is it lawful to do good or to do harm on the sabbath, to save life or to kill?"

Jesus asks. His opponents refuse to dialogue. They apparently want to catch Jesus on a point of Jewish Law, not something limited to the oral tradition of the Pharisees but something to outrage religious leaders of all factions. The Sabbath law in Exodus states: "Whoever does any work on the sabbath day shall be put to death" (Exod 31:15).

Jesus asks, "Is it lawful to do good on the Sabbath?" Such questions have been debated at length. A widely accepted standard was that if this man would die that day if he were not helped, the law allows one to minister to him even on the Sabbath. It is clear that healing the man's withered hand is not necessary in that sense. But the leaders do not even offer this. They offer no frame of reference, no Scripture for interpretation. Jesus knows he has been put on the spot and it will be costly. He is angered at the leaders' absolute refusal to talk about what is right to do. The leaders are not open to hearing something new.

Jesus does not back down. What he does is consistent with what he has done before, consistent with his claim that the Sabbath was made out of God's love for humans, not to enslave humans to the Sabbath. He does not explain himself here. He simply speaks, "Put forth your hand." The man with the withered hand puts his hand forth and it is restored.

There will be debates over whether Jesus actually worked in doing this act of power. What did he do? A person is allowed to speak on the Sabbath. Did the man work? He raised his hand to be healed. What is clear is that Jesus healed, or that God healed the man's hand at Jesus' bidding. So can God work on the Sabbath, God's day of rest?

Who are the Herodians? They work for Herod Antipas, the son of Herod the Great who is now tetrarch of Galilee and Perea. One step lower than a king, he was appointed by Augustus Caesar and is responsible to Rome for all matters in his kingdom. He imprisoned John the Baptist. One suspects that if Jesus were to openly proclaim himself Messiah, the king of Israel, Herod would quickly want him silenced. Perhaps the Pharisees who left the synagogue with the Herodians had something like that in mind.

Preaching the kingdom of God might sound solemnly religious but it inevitably reaches into social and political issues as well, practical matters of justice and right living. In this manner the kingdom of God broke in on the man with a withered hand. Jesus did not humiliate him by postponing his healing until sunset. Jesus could expect serious repercussions for healing this man before these witnesses in the synagogue on the Sabbath, yet he went ahead to relieve this man of a burden that he had lived with. It was a costly act for Jesus, a redemptive act of love.

7 Jesus departed with his disciples to the sea, and a great multitude from Galilee followed him; 8 hearing all that he

"Follow Me."

> was doing, they came to him in great numbers from Judea, Jerusalem, Idumea, beyond the Jordan, and the region around Tyre and Sidon. 9 He told his disciples to have a boat ready for him because of the crowd, so that they would not crush him; 10 for he had cured many, so that all who had diseases pressed upon him to touch him. 11 Whenever the unclean spirits saw him, they fell down before him and shouted, "You are the Son of God!" 12 But he sternly ordered them not to make him known.

Jesus withdraws to the Sea of Galilee for some respite. The synagogue at Capernaum has called Jesus into question, raising questions about his understanding of the Law, questioning what he is doing. Jesus retreats with his disciples, followed by a great crowd.

Jesus has invited many to follow him. Mark gives the impression that the crowds who follow him are increasing in size. The evening after that first Sabbath "the whole city" of Capernaum gathered (1:33). After preaching throughout Galilee (1:39) the crowds came "so that Jesus could no longer go into a town" (1:45). Now, after a series of actions and statements that challenge the purity code (2:1—3.6), the crowds are gathering from all over Israel and from foreign lands (3:7–8).

Do the people come just to listen? No. So many rush in to touch him and be healed that Jesus could be crushed; crowd control problems come up. The unclean spirits shout out, "You are the Son of God!" (3:11). Again Jesus commands them sternly not to make him known.

Many who follow are *am haaretz* (people of the land), the country folk, the sinners, for whom the open invitation to repent and to enter the kingdom of God is good news because they have long since failed to meet the purity code. Some of these people saw, or heard about, what happened in the synagogue. They may need to rethink their position, they want to know where Jesus is leading them.

There have been previous retreats. After baptism the Spirit drove Jesus into the wilderness (1:12). This was followed by a clear statement of Jesus' teaching (1:14–15). After the first Sabbath in Capernaum Jesus went to a deserted place to pray, followed by his statement of purpose (1:35, 38). Will the mission be further defined this time around?

> 13 He went up to the mountain and called to him those whom he wanted, and they came to him. 14 And he appointed twelve, whom he also named apostles, to be with

> him, and to be sent out to proclaim the message, 15 and to have authority to cast out demons. 16 So he appointed the twelve: Simon (to whom he gave the name Peter); 17 James son of Zebedee and John the brother of James (to whom he gave the name Boanerges, that is, Sons of Thunder); 18 and Andrew, and Phillip, and Bartholomew, and Matthew, and Thomas, and James son of Alphaeus, and Thaddaeus, and Simon the Cananaean, 19 and Judas Iscariot, who betrayed him.

The four fishermen encountered in chapter 1 are named as a group. Simon Peter is first, his brother Andrew fourth on the list. James and John are given a nickname, Boanerges, Sons of Thunder. Their father Zebedee must have had a fisherman's famous temper. Then out of a larger group of followers, eight additional disciples are mentioned by name. These twelve are chosen to be intimate companions of Jesus, a select group that he designates as apostles. The word "apostle" comes from *apo*, a preposition that means from, away from, or out; and the verb *stello*, to send, to place, to set out in order as an army. Jesus intends that they should learn enough from him to help carry on the task of proclaiming the good news, repentance, and the kingdom of God; even be given the power to heal the sick and to cast out demons. They are provided with Jesus' authority to do these tasks. Jesus is confident that he has not misunderstood his mission. He is ready to share his mission with a circle of companions.

From this point forward these twelve receive a good deal of attention in Mark's narrative. We should note that in setting the twelve apart like this a distinction between insiders and outsiders begins to be made.

In the next episode Jesus goes home, perhaps to Nazareth because his family shows up. Such a crowd gathers that he and others with him can't even eat. His family comes near. They may want to dissuade him from the course he has embarked on: to get him to step aside, to change his mind, to repent, to lead a normal life, to stop alienating the religious authorities. In fact the authorities from Jerusalem are aggressively interrogating him.

> Then he went home; 20 and the crowd came together again, so that they could not even eat. 21 When his family heard it, they went out to restrain him, for people were saying, "He has gone out of his mind." 22 And the scribes who came down from Jerusalem said, "He has Beelzebul, and by the ruler of the demons he casts out demons." 23 And he called them to him, and spoke to them in parables, "How can Satan cast out Satan? 24 If a kingdom is divided against

> itself, that kingdom cannot stand. 25 And if a house is divided against itself, that house will not be able to stand. 26 And if Satan has risen up against himself and is divided, he cannot stand, but his end has come. 27 But no one can enter a strong man's house and plunder his property without first tying up the strong man; then indeed the house can be plundered.
>
> 28 "Truly I tell you, people will be forgiven for their sins and whatever blasphemies they utter; 29 but whoever blasphemes against the Holy Spirit can never have forgiveness, but is guilty of an eternal sin"— 30 for they had said, "He has an unclean spirit."

Why such a ferocious attack on Jesus? Word has gotten back to Jerusalem that Jesus is drawing crowds—the Jesus who welcomes people who do not observe the Law, who heals on the Sabbath, who defies religious correction, who claims he is lord of the Sabbath, who claims authority as the Son of Man to forgive sins. The facts themselves accuse him. He sounds like a would-be messiah without making the direct claim. Can such a man be called righteous? He must be mad! Or he is possessed! The Jerusalem scribes now go on the offensive. They accuse him of leading people astray. They raise a legitimate question about the source of Jesus' power but phrase it in such a way as to try to undermine Jesus' influence with the crowds.

Jesus' response is worth considering. He calls them to himself. The Greek verb Mark uses is *proskaleomai*, to summon, to invite, to call to oneself. The same verb was used in 3:13 when Jesus summoned the twelve disciples to him. Jesus' response is not simply a defensive maneuver. It is an appeal to the scribes and to the crowd to listen to him. He remains in an inviting mode. He beckons them to come, follow.

Jesus answers the accusation that he is a man possessed by Beelzebul, the Lord of the Flies, with parables. With three images he points out the self-destruction that comes when a household, a kingdom, or even Satan sets itself in contention against itself. If Satan casts out Satan's demons he will destroy himself. The clear implication is that in casting out spirits from persons identified as demon-possessed, Jesus is already exercising some power over Satan's kingdom, not Satan destroying himself.

We get advice on how to plunder a strong man's house. Bind up the strong man first. Again Jesus implies that the strong man is Satan and that in casting out demons Jesus is at least beginning to overpower Satan.

Then Jesus turns subtly on the scribes from Jerusalem to warn them that blasphemy against the Holy Spirit of God is a very serious offense. They should take care whose Spirit they call Satanic. He challenges them to pause and see that his work is good, is holy, and is from God.

Mark paints this encounter as a victory for Jesus because the Jerusalem scribes have no rebuttal. But if the point is to win over the other side the result is about a draw. In Mark's narrative, however, the overall effect of this encounter is to clarify Mark's thesis that the power of God has come on earth, that in the deeds of Jesus we have seen at least small victories over Satan.

This passage gives us details for Mark's understanding of Satan. In 1:13 Satan "tempted" Jesus, but it was not quite clear whether he was testing Jesus to make him strong or setting out to defeat Jesus. Here Jesus calls Satan a strong man whom he must bind up, an evil opponent over whom Jesus exercises power when he heals and casts out demons. The language is concrete and immediate. This impression will be confirmed in the parable of the sower (Mark 4:15), another time Jesus mentions Satan. Satan is the bird who snatches the seed from a listener, an outside power who works to have his way against the sower. Mark's Satan is not the accuser in God's court, nor even "evil in the abstract," but an active antagonist with whom Jesus contends.

> **31 Then his mother and his brothers came; and standing outside, they sent to him and called him. 32 A crowd was sitting around him; and they said to him, "Your mother and your brothers and sisters are outside, asking for you. 33 And he replied, "Who are my mother and my brothers?" 34 And looking at those who sat around him, he said, "Here are my mother and my brothers! 35 Whoever does the will of God is my brother and sister and mother."**

People start telling Jesus that his mother, his brothers, and his sisters are outside calling for him. "Who are my mother and my brothers?" Jesus asks. This response may shock the crowd. Has he insulted his mother and family? Is Jesus is disowning his very kin? But people have been whispering that Jesus has gone crazy. His mother wants to rescue him from the hot spot, from attack by the acclaimed scribes of Jerusalem. Jesus will not concede, by an act that takes him off the hot spot, even the hint that he is not in full possession of his faculties. He knows what he is doing and will stand his ground with the best scholars of the Law.

"Follow Me."

But in the excitement we must not miss a very important characterization Jesus provides of what he sees himself doing. It rounds out his answer to the attack of the scribes. Jesus affirms those sitting around him, those closest to him, women with children and men who came in early to hear him: "Here are my mother, and my brother, and sister: whoever does the will of God."

Mark Chapter 4

EVEN IF WE GRANT that Jesus won the argument with the scribes who accused him of being demon-possessed, it should be clear that Jesus' position remains precarious. Note the predicament for those who would follow him. With clashes like these with respected religious leaders, how should we think of Jesus' kingdom of God? In what direction are followers to go? Does Jesus expect his followers to do the things that he does? What should we answer when people ask, "Who is this Jesus who walks before you?"

When we encounter Jesus once again in Mark, we find that he is back somewhere on the shore of the Sea of Galilee. The crowd this time is so large that Jesus moves to a boat to teach from just offshore. As he has on previous occasions, he speaks in parables. In a parable, a figure of speech is used to compare one reality with a similar but different reality. It can be a proverb, a metaphor, or a story. It requires the listener to actively work with the comparison.

> 4 Again he began to teach beside the sea. Such a very large crowd gathered around him that he got into a boat on the sea and sat there, while the whole crowd was beside the sea on the land. 2 He began to teach them many things in parables, and in his teaching he said to them: 3 "Listen! A sower went out to sow. 4 And as he sowed, some seed fell on the path, and the birds came and ate it up. 5 Other seed fell on rocky ground, where it did not have much soil, and it sprang up quickly, since it had no depth of soil. 6 And when the sun rose, it was scorched; and since it had no root, it withered away. 7 Other seed fell among thorns, and the thorns grew up and choked it, and it yielded no grain. 8 Other seed fell into good soil and brought forth grain, growing up and increasing and yielding thirty and sixty

> **and a hundredfold." 9 And he said, "Let anyone with ears to hear listen!"**

Listen! This translates an emphatic phrase. Jesus is probably speaking Aramaic or Hebrew in which a verb is characteristically repeated twice for emphasis, once in the present perfect, once as a command: *Shimu Shamoa.* Upon hearing, hear this! While you're listening, listen to this! Pay attention!

Let's try to hear this parable in the way the original listeners heard it, without the interpretation the disciples get later. Jesus sits in the boat to tell us a story, a story about a sower who sows seed and depending on where the seed falls there are different results. This one has relevance to what is happening around us. Listen.

Isn't Jesus telling this story on himself? Jesus is throwing out seed and the seed is received differently by different listeners. This is what happens in all his encounters. And the parable concludes with a great harvest. Is Jesus saying something like this, that the news he has been preaching and enacting before us is indeed good news that is going to bear a great yield? The overall result will be an abundant harvest despite the fact that some people have rebuffed him. Listeners should not get bogged down in the rebuffs. We should keep our eye on the seed and rejoice in the harvest that is promised.

> **10 When he was alone, those who were around him along with the twelve asked him about the parables. 11 And he said to them, "To you has been given the secret of the kingdom of God, but for those outside, everything comes in parables; 12 in order that**
>
> **'they may indeed look, but not perceive,**
>
> **and may indeed listen, but not understand;**
>
> **so that they may not turn again and be forgiven.'"**

Note that at verse 10, Mark interrupts Jesus' parabolic discourse and jumps ahead to a time when the disciples can catch Jesus alone after most of the crowd has dispersed. They inquire about the parables. Jesus responds first with the puzzling statement just quoted and we get his interpretation of the parable of the sower. Because the puzzles can apply to all the parables, in fact to the entire Gospel, we will examine Jesus' answer and his interpretation of this parable of the sower after the end of the parabolic discourse following verse 33. But for now, we shall simply take Jesus' words on his own parable and continue with his sermon of parables.

> 13 And he said to them, "Do you not understand this parable? Then how will you understand all the parables? 14 The sower sows the word. 15 These are the ones on the path where the word is sown: when they hear, Satan immediately comes and takes away the word that is sown in them. 16 And these are the ones sown on rocky ground: when they hear the word, they immediately receive it with joy. 17 But they have no root, and endure only for a while; then, when trouble or persecution arises on account of the word, immediately they fall away. 18 And others are those sown among the thorns: these are the ones who hear the word, 19 but the cares of the world, and the lure of wealth, and the desire for other things come in and choke the word, and it yields nothing. 20 And these are the ones sown on the good soil: they hear the word and accept it and bear fruit, thirty and sixty and a hundred fold."

We might note that the additional details Jesus brings to this parable add an element of judgment that was not obvious at first hearing.

A second parable invites a touch of humor.

> 21 He said to them, "Is a lamp brought in to be put under the bushel basket, or under the bed, and not on the lampstand? 22 For there is nothing hidden, except to be disclosed; nor is anything secret, except to come to light. 23 Let anyone with ears to hear listen!"

In this parable Jesus asks a question that will delight every child in the crowd who is listening. A common clay lamp is brought into a dark room. Do you place it under a basket? Do you put it under the bed? And with the laughter of children the adults can realize that the teacher may be telling this one on himself as well. The oil lamp is made to bring light in public places. The lamp holder comes in with a light that he will not hide.

There is a context for these parables in Mark. It is the question made urgent for the crowd by that last round of events in Nazareth. Jesus, why have you gotten yourself into such a terrible bind with powerful religious leaders? Why have you healed people on the Sabbath? Why have you forgiven, and claimed that the Son of Man has power to forgive? What are you doing? In such a context the parable suggests that the various things Jesus has been doing radiate from a light source that he brings with him. He does these things to convey a certain truth that he embodies. Jesus enters as with a lamp with a burning wick. The image here is not of a modern spotlight but of a common clay oil lamp that gives out light enough to show the faces and body outlines of persons close by in a dark room. Jesus comes in with a message that challenges the settled order of his time and our own accepted order. The kingdom of God is near at hand. His actions and his teaching are all meant to illuminate this truth. This is the task for which he was anointed. A man with an oil lamp is entering the room.

Like the metaphors of the cloth patches and the wineskins, this parable is suggestive rather than directly spelling out details of the allusion for us. We could note, however, that the word *hina* occurs four times in the Greek telling of this parable. *Hina* means roughly "in order to." Our NRSV translation uses simply "to" and slides over the second, "to be placed on the lampstand." In the next verse the phrase "except to" twice expresses a use of the same word. The repeated emphasis of an act done in order to accomplish something suggests how intentionally the act is done. And in the double emphasis on disclosure in the second verse Jesus interprets his parable by saying that what is only alluded to here, what is half hidden now, will be brought to light.

> **24 And he said to them, "Pay attention to what you hear; the measure you give will be the measure you get, and still more will be given you. 25 For to those who have, more will be given; and from those who have nothing, even what they have will be taken away."**

How shall we listen? What should we attend to here? What is the good news in these words? We have heard the preaching, we have seen Jesus healing, we have noted his interest in individual lives. Jesus is saying: this is what God's love is like. See it in what I do. Hear it in my words. Give to others as I give to you. Learn from the Spirit that flows through me. If you give with such a measure, your measure will be more than replenished.

The saying ends with a division between persons who are willing to partake of and share God's Spirit, and others who will not. The life you lead will be the life you get. Pay attention!

> **26 He also said, "The kingdom of God is as if someone would scatter seed on the ground, 27 and would sleep and rise night and day, and the seed would sprout and grow, he**

> does not know how. 28 The earth produces of itself, first the stalk, then the head, then the full grain in the head. 29 But when the grain is ripe, at once he goes in with his sickle, because the harvest has come."

We come now to the two parables told explicitly about the kingdom of God, about the realm and sovereignty of God. God's kingdom is like someone, you, me, or another, who scatters seed. The kingdom seed is planted. How the seed grows we do not know. The seed comes into individual lives. We should not worry over how little seems to take place or how long it takes to grow. Over such matters we have no control. We might as well sleep or rise or tend to other things. But when the grain is finally seen swaying ripe, blowing in the breeze, we will know what to do. The time of harvest is arrived.

Contrast this image with the kingdom of David and of Solomon. That was an earthly rule based on military strength, on compulsion, and on wealth. These kings put forth forces to be seen, heralded by loud trumpets to make people tremble. Or put it in context of the practical question of the day: should one support the violent overthrow of a foreign oppressor? This parable places Jesus, among Pharisees, nearer to the school of Hillel than the school of Shammai, disciples of a second important Jewish teacher and contemporary of Hillel. Hillel was inclined to leave those matters in God's hands and live under Roman rule as long as Jews were allowed to study and live the Torah. In contrast, the school of Shammai was less willing to put up with Rome and sought an active and sometimes revolutionary role in seeking to free the Jews and bring in God's kingdom by force.[1]

The parable shows Jesus single-mindedly focused on God's kingdom and God's work. One may plant a kingdom seed but how it grows is not ours to control. The kingdom of God comes quietly, slowly, almost unseen. It comes without coercion. It is meant for our true freedom. It is God's realm at work, not ours. It bursts out here and there, where we may least expect it.

> 30 He also said, "With what can we compare the kingdom of God, or what parable will we use for it? 31 It is like a mustard seed, which, when sown upon the ground, is the smallest of all the seeds on earth; 32 yet when it is sown it grows up and becomes the greatest of all shrubs, and puts

---

1. For a study of first-century Pharisees and rebellion against Rome, see Wright, *New Testament and the People of God*, 157–203.

> **forth large branches, so that the birds of the air can make nests in its shade."**

God's realm is like a very small seed that grows into a large bush with much foliage, green leaves to shade all kinds of birds, a sovereignty to minister to and bless all creation. It puts one in the mood of God's promise to Abraham: I will bless you. I will make of you a great nation, and in you all the families of the earth shall be blessed (Gen 12:2–3).

This, then, is one way to read Jesus' parable teaching in Mark 4. But the parables come right out of life. They can be interpreted in many ways and applied with slight nuances to situations across the ages. They provide puzzles that bring us back to them to be challenged, and to be refreshed. We should play with them. Why speak in parables to the crowds? Because they give us a chance to hear and hear again, to see and see again. It is the touch of a master teacher.

> **33 With many such parables he spoke the word to them, as they were able to hear it; 34 he did not speak to them except in parables, but he explained everything in private to his disciples.**

We come now to what Jesus teaches his disciples, after the crowd he spoke to in parables from the boat has dispersed. Notice how Jesus himself draws the distinction between insiders and outsiders. At the same time Jesus challenges his disciples with one of the most puzzling statements in the entire book. We get a slightly different flavor to his words by taking up from Mark 4:10 in the King James Version:

> **10 And when he was alone, they that were about him with the twelve asked of him the parable. 11 And he said unto them, Unto you it is given to know the mystery of the kingdom of God; but unto them that are without, all** *these* **things are done in parables; 12 That seeing they may see, and not perceive; and hearing they may hear, and not understand; lest at any time they should be converted, and** *their* **sins should be forgiven them. (KJV)**

Jesus speaks here of the mystery of the kingdom of God. The NRSV speaks of the secret of the kingdom of God. The Greek (*mysterion*) is rightfully translated either way. But Jesus immediately continues with the disturbing thought that the parables are told, *hina*, "in order that" (NRSV) or simply "that" (KJV), the secret be kept from outsiders. The parables are told, *hina*, "so that" outsiders must fail to see or fail to understand something that would lead them to turn from their sins and be forgiven. This phrase introduces the fifth use of the *hina* phrase in this chapter, which sets up a tremendous tension with the other four uses of that phrase found in the parable of the lampholder. Whereas the lampholder enters with the oil lamp burning in order to shed light in a dark room, here it sounds like Jesus speaks in parables in order to keep the mystery of the light hidden.

Would Jesus tell parables to hide his teaching? Surely Jesus is not speaking in parables to keep the crowds from hearing him, to keep them from repenting and being forgiven. That would contradict his message from the outset of his ministry (Mark 1:14–15, 38). What then can Jesus mean in making this statement? We shall deal first with the *hina* phrase and then come back to the question about a secret of the kingdom.

Jesus quotes from God's commissioning of the prophet Isaiah here, see Isaiah 6:1–13. When Isaiah stood in the temple facing the Lord God seated on a high throne, he was overcome by his own sin and cried out, "I am lost, for I am a man of unclean lips and I live among a people of unclean lips" (JB).[2] A seraph who had been praising God touched Isaiah's lips with a live coal from the altar, and said, "This coal has touched your lips, your sin is taken away, your iniquity is purged." Isaiah then heard God's voice ask, "Whom shall I send? Who will be our messenger?" Isaiah volunteered, and God commissioned him using the same words that Jesus used in telling the parables, *Shimu Shamoa*: "Say to this people,

> 9 'Hear and hear again, but do not understand;
>   see and see again, but do not perceive.'
> 10 Make the heart of this people gross, its ears dull;
>   shut its eyes so that it will not see with its eyes,
>   hear with its ears, understand with its heart,
>   and be converted and healed." (Isa 6:9–10, JB)

The words are as puzzling when spoken to Isaiah as they are on Jesus' lips six centuries later. Isaiah himself had just repented and been forgiven. He knew his people needed to repent in God's presence. The instructions suggest that people will not listen to a further call to repentance. "Until when, Lord?" Isaiah asked. "Until towns have been laid waste and deserted," was

---

2. The Isaiah quotations in this section come from the *Jerusalem Bible*.

"Follow Me."

the reply. Isaiah was to persist in his mission even if most people rejected him, even if the Jews were taken into exile. However, a promise was tucked in at the end of the commissioning: a remnant of the people, "a holy seed," would remain faithful to God (Isa 6:13).

Isaiah went on to call his people to repent and to put God first in their lives. He instructed Ahaz, king in Jerusalem, to stop his political plotting and to trust God even in his conduct of Judah's foreign policy. Isaiah followed this up with warnings about destruction if Ahaz should fail to respond. When Ahaz demurred, Isaiah foretold that a son would be born in the house of David, Immanuel, another king who would rule with justice and integrity, who would be a great light in the darkness (Isa 7:1–17; 9:1–7). Isaiah warned all his people of God's impending judgment, of destruction and exile if they did not repent (Isa 9:8—10:4).

Isaiah did not limit God's call to repentance with its warnings to the descendants of Abraham alone. He proclaimed a similar message to the surrounding nations: Babylon, Assyria, Philistia, Moab, Damascus, Cush, Egypt, Tyre, and Sidon. He warned them of the day of God's judgment on all the inhabitants of the earth.

Thus, even if Isaiah understood God to be speaking with irony in the first words of his commissioning, he certainly took the instructions seriously. Perhaps he heard some hint of the resistance he should realistically expect. Isaiah interpreted the words as God's strident call to repentance, to conversion and healing, and as a warning of great destruction if many refused to listen. But a remnant of Jews and of all peoples, a holy seed, a repentant and obedient community, would be faithful to God. That was God's promise.

It seems to me that Jesus hints here that, like Isaiah, he too must persist despite resistance to his message in various quarters. Jesus' sermon theme recapitulates Isaiah's experience before God: Repent and be forgiven. God's kingdom welcomes you. Jesus certainly emphasizes the good news in God's invitation and usually downplays the destruction that sin brings with it. His parables in Mark have emphasized the blessing and the victory that comes through the mystery of God's grace which lies beyond our control, outside the focus of our vision. But when the disciples and others close to him ask him, "Why do you teach the people in parables?" Jesus answers with God's instructions to Isaiah.[3] This suggests that he, like Isaiah, will persist in his call for repentance despite the cost.

And this is the moment with his disciples when Jesus interprets his own parable about different receptions to the seed sown by the sower. The quote from Isaiah may remind the disciples that the good news Jesus brings includes a call to repentance. Such a call suggests a warning judgment that choosing evil brings destruction. In my estimate, after this Isaiah lesson, there is no avoiding the hint of judgment implicit in the parable of the sower whose seed lands in various places. The news of the kingdom bears good fruit to those who make it their own, but those who reject it are in peril. The invitation to enter and become part of God's kingdom is meant to be a serious gift to reckon with.

For his part, in retelling his parable Jesus immediately identifies the seed that the sower sows as "the word," *ton logon* (4:14). At the end of this parabolic discourse Mark tells us that "with many such parables he spoke the word to them" (4:33). On a previous occasion, when people crowded into that house in Capernaum, Mark said that Jesus "was speaking the word" to them (2:2). Here Jesus uses *ton logon*, the word, to identify his own message, the good news he brings in its various expressions. And indeed, the various places where the seed lands in the parable represent different human responses to his good news. In some places it is as if the message were immediately snatched away. Other people accept it as good news with joy but lose their focus on it when trouble or persecution comes because of the word, and fall away. Still others listen to and hear the word, but the cares of this life, or the desire for acclaim, or for riches, or some other yearning, chokes out the word. The seed in such cases bears little fruit. But there are those who accept the good news in its power and continue to live in it, who will bear many forms of abundant fruit. Spelled out explicitly in this way, we encounter the judgment implicit in this parable. Embrace Jesus' invitation into the kingdom of God and receive its rich blessing. But if we

---

3. Jeremias provides a specific solution to the *hina* problem by dealing with the Greek. Mark's paraphrase of Isaiah (6:9–10) follows neither the Hebrew nor the Septuagint (Greek) text but agrees with the Targum, the Aramaic version commonly used in the synagogues. The troubling word *hina*, "in order that," is therefore part of the quote from Isaiah, God's word to Isaiah, not the direct expression of Jesus' purpose in telling the parables. Jeremias, *Parables of Jesus*, 15–17.

"Follow Me."

shun the word or push it aside we should expect to bear the fruit that our alternative choices will bring.

What are we to do with that judgment? We like to apply a judgment about reception of the word to the characters in the book. What seed falls along the path must fall to some scribes, we say, or to Pharisees who resist Jesus. The thorny ground may represent the rich man we will meet. Persons who are healed have a faith that bears fruit. Sounds like good soil. The disciples receive the word with joy. But from now on Mark will show them constantly falling. Are they meant for rocky ground? We are to learn from the persons who interact with Jesus. But if we stop here, judging others only, if we end up thinking that some people are simply good soil and others bad, we will entirely miss Jesus' focus, the primary thrust of Jesus' ministry!

What is the good news preached by Jesus? Repent and become good earth. The seed, the word, is offered as good news for Pharisees if they will receive it; offered to synagogue leaders as well as to fishermen. His voice brings an invitation to the listener. We are to judge ourselves and apply the parable to ourselves, not condemn others. We can choose the good news. It is a freeing news for grave sinners, good news even for disciples thrust into demanding situations, slipping and unsure of themselves. Become good soil. The news is proclaimed to people who are alive, still making decisions at risk.

But there remains more to be explored in Jesus' answer to the disciples' questions about his parables (4:10). What is the *mysterion*, the secret or mystery of the kingdom of God? There is a motif we have encountered in Mark that maintains a tension throughout the book that is similar to the tension between the two uses of *hina* in chapter 4 (parables to hide a truth vs. parables to bring in light). This motif involves what is often called the messianic secret. On the one hand Jesus has not allowed anyone to proclaim that he is the Messiah. Time and again Jesus has publicly silenced an "unclean spirit" who claimed to know his identity. On the other hand, the confidence and authority with which Jesus moves is extraordinary. As his Jewish listeners contemplate his righteous life, his teachings, his acts of wonder and mercy, they will ask, "Is this Jesus the Messiah, the one who is to come and free us?" The matter is open to be seen by all, yet it is insistently kept hidden. Why? Might this provide a clue to the secret of the kingdom

Mark Chapter 4

of God in Mark, a key to a mystery of the kingdom that disciples are given? (4:11)[4]

We know that Mark is quite willing to leave his readers with unanswered questions to struggle with. On the other hand, might it be the case that Mark has intertwined these two mysteries, the secret of the kingdom and the secret of the Messiah, these two sets of unresolved tensions, on purpose, as if they are in some manner parallel to or interrelated with one another? If Mark is doing this on purpose, we must continue reading this Gospel to see if and where we can find a solution to resolve these puzzles. For now, however, let us return to that day when Jesus spoke to the crowd in numerous parables from a boat just offshore.

> **35 On that day, when evening had come, he said to them, "Let us go across to the other side." 36 And leaving the crowd behind, they took him with them in the boat, just as he was. Other boats were with him. 37 A great windstorm arose, and the waves beat into the boat, so that the boat was already being swamped. 38 But he was in the stern, asleep on the cushion; and they woke him up and said to him, "Teacher, do you not care that we are perishing?" 39 He woke up and rebuked the wind, and said to the sea, "Peace! Be still!" Then the wind ceased, and there was a dead calm. 40 He said to them, "Why are you afraid? Have you still no faith?" 41 And they were filled with great awe and said to one another, "Who then is this, that even the wind and the sea obey him?"**

As a fisherman, I note that the disciples hold off their fears for some considerable time before waking Jesus. Perhaps the boat was overloaded to begin with, the sort of thing you notice after the wind picks up. The wind has gotten so strong that waves are breaking over the gunnels. The boat will be swamped and sink. Such is the normal course of nature. The disciples get desperate while Jesus sleeps soundly, exhausted, in the stern of the boat.

---

4. Joel Marcus in *The Mystery of the Kingdom of God* makes a tightly argued scholarly case for the claim that the mystery of the kingdom found in the parable of the sower, in all the parables of Mark 4, and implicit in the entire Gospel, is that while the kingdom of God is already come and is bearing its yield, evil has not yet been eradicated from the world. Contrary to expectation, the kingdom is at present accompanied by opposition and failure. The kingdom is yet to come in its full glory. Marcus develops one answer to the question. But there are other solutions.

"Follow Me."

They turn to wake him. We can hear the fearful edge in their voices: "Don't you care if we perish?"

And we hear Jesus' stunning question, "Why are you afraid? Have you still no faith?"

The word "afraid" translates the Greek adjective *deiloi*, "timid or fearful," which is used only here in Mark. "Why are you timid?" Jesus asks. "Where is your courage?" What faith is it that Jesus wishes they had? How should that translate into our lives? The disciples have some faith. After all, they turned to Jesus for help. Does Jesus think *they* should have calmed the sea? Surely not. Jesus directs his words at their fear. Is it that Jesus wants the disciples to trust God, to know that they can trust God without fear even if they are all to drown this very night? Is there more for us to learn by watching Jesus act in faith?

As surprising as his chiding, Jesus brings in some of God's control over the natural world. At his words the wind subdues. "Peace! Be still!" It is a version of what he is saying to the disciples issued in the form of a command rather than a question. The sea flattens out in a great calm.

The wind and the sea obey him. Mark uses the Greek verb *hupakouo*, "to obey," twice: here and in 1:27, when the demonic spirit abandoned that first man in the synagogue. *Hupakouo* means obedient hearing, that of a doorman who listens for the knock at the door and opens it. It is made up by combining the preposition *hupo*, "under," with the verb *akouo*, "to listen," the Greek verb used repeatedly in this chapter and throughout Mark. The wind and the sea listen and are calmed.

The disciples, by contrast, are not so readily calmed. Mark uses both a passive of the verb *phobeo*, (to be frightened, to be terrified), and the noun *phobos*, (fear, fright, dread, terror), to describe the disciples. They were frightened with a great fear, mingled with awe. The moment ripples through them with lingering intensity: "Who can this man be?"

Mark leaves us with the disciples' question.

Mark Chapter 5

THIS CHAPTER RECORDS THREE detailed accounts of Jesus' healing power, and each account is related to us in long paragraphs. A boat with Jesus and some disciples lands on the east side of the Sea of Galilee in the region of the Decapolis, ten Greek cities. It is pagan territory for the Jews although there are diaspora Jews who live here. There is a herd of pigs nearby. Jews consider pigs to be an unclean meat and would not raise pigs. The Gerasene demoniac is found living in a cemetery. That fact alone may count against him as unclean by Jewish standards. This man may be filthy, he probably hasn't bathed for weeks, and he is filled with an unclean spirit. Jesus ventures into foreign territories.

> **5** They came to the other side of the sea, to the country of the Gerasenes. 2 And when he had stepped out of the boat, immediately a man out of the tombs with an unclean spirit met him. 3 He lived among the tombs; and no one could restrain him any more, even with a chain; 4 for he had often been restrained with shackles and chains, but the chains he wrenched apart, and the shackles he broke in pieces; and no one had the strength to subdue him. 5 Night and day among the tombs and on the mountains he was always howling and bruising himself with stones. 6 When he saw Jesus from a distance, he ran and bowed down before him; 7 and he shouted at the top of his voice, "What have you to do with me, Jesus, Son of the Most High God? I adjure you by God, do not torment me." 8 For he had said to him, "Come out of the man, you unclean spirit!" 9 Then Jesus asked him, "What is your name?" He replied, "My name is Legion, for we are many." 10 He begged him earnestly not to send them out of the country. 11 Now there on the

> hillside a great herd of swine was feeding; 12 and the unclean spirits begged him, "Send us into the swine; let us enter them." 13 So he gave them permission. And the unclean spirits came out and entered the swine; and the herd, numbering about two thousand, rushed down the steep bank into the sea, and were drowned in the sea.

The demoniac is very strong. Mark tells us twice that no one had the power to subdue him. He has torn their chains apart and shattered shackles. An outcast, he frequents mountains and graveyards. No one has been able to help him. Tormented, he cries out night and day and bruises himself with stones.

This man runs from a distance toward Jesus and throws himself at his feet, crying loudly for mercy. "I know who you are, Jesus, Son of the Most High God." He pleads earnestly with him, "Do not torment me!"

Jesus talks with him, already quieting things down. Then Jesus asks him, "What is your name?"

He replied, "My name is Legion, for we are many." A Roman military division of about 6,000 men makes up a legion. The demoniac now goes through a certain bargaining with Jesus concerning the disposition of his evil spirits. With an act that grants him a special dignity, Jesus honors his request. "Don't drive us out of the country. Send us into that nearby herd of swine." Jesus permits it. And to the astonishment of any onlookers, the swine rush down a steep bank and are drowned in the Sea of Galilee.

Jesus ministers to this Gerasene tenderly, face to face. It reminds us of the thief in the parable who tied up the strong man, but this strong man was one that no one, including himself, had power to control. Jesus frees him! The man becomes coherent, the disciples find an untattered garment with which to clothe him, and he tells them his story.

There are social costs in this story. The swineherds ran off. They must notify the owners about losing the pigs and may fear punishment, so they broadcast the story in the country and city. If enough persons come to know it, they will not have to face the owners alone. And, as we might expect, the owners of the herd soon rush in, panting. Two thousand pigs is a significant financial loss.

> 14 The swineherds ran off and told it in the city and in the country. Then people came to see what it was that had happened. 15 They came to Jesus and saw the demoniac sitting there, clothed and in his right mind, the very man

> who had had the legion; and they were afraid. 16 Those who had seen what had happened to the demoniac and to the swine reported it. 17 Then they began to beg Jesus to leave their neighborhood. 18 As he was getting into the boat, the man who had been possessed by demons begged him that he might be with him. 19 But Jesus refused, and said to him, "Go home to your friends, and tell them how much the Lord has done for you, and what mercy he has shown you. 20 And he went away and began to proclaim in the Decapolis how much Jesus had done for him; and everyone was amazed.

We find echoes of Jesus' early ministry in Galilee. A man, a sinner, one possessed, cries out in recognition when he sees God's power in Jesus. Jesus in response brings him healing, forgiveness, and restoration. The kingdom of God is offered to a man who is not a Jew, on foreign soil. But it is interesting that when he asks to follow Jesus, to go to the other side in the boat with him, Jesus sends him back to his own people instead, giving him a different task. This is the unforeseen beginning of Jesus' ministry to gentiles.

Jesus returns to the western, Jewish, side of the Sea of Galilee.

> 21 When Jesus had crossed again in the boat to the other side, a great crowd gathered around him; and he was by the sea. 22 Then one of the leaders of the synagogue named Jairus came and, when he saw him, fell at his feet 23 and begged him repeatedly, "My little daughter is at the point of death. Come and lay your hands on her, so that she may be made well, and live." 24 So he went with him.

There are two stories here, one inside the other. The outer story begins with Jairus, a synagogue leader who falls at Jesus' feet. Whatever reservations Jairus may have had over Jesus' conflicts with synagogue leaders is blown aside by Jairus' desperate need: his daughter is close to death. Jairus pleads for Jesus to come, touch his daughter, and heal her. They start for Jairus' home.

This walk is suddenly interrupted when Jesus stops and looks around at the crowd following with them. "Who touched me?" Jesus asks. "I felt a certain power go through me. Who touched me?" And we get the story of an unnamed woman's desperate search for healing. Her bleeding makes her ritually unclean. Thus Jairus, one of the few comers called by name, a

"Follow Me."

recognized Law-observant Jew, gets his paths crossed with this woman. He is forced to stop, wait, listen to Jesus, and watch this scene play out.

> **And a large crowd followed him and pressed in on him. 25 Now there was a woman who had been suffering from hemorrhages for twelve years. 26 She had endured much under many physicians, and had spent all she had; and she was no better, but rather grew worse. 27 She had heard about Jesus, and came up behind him in the crowd and touched his cloak, 28 for she said, "If I but touch his clothes, I will be made well." 29 Immediately her hemorrhage stopped; and she felt in her body that she was healed of her disease. 30 Immediately aware that power had gone forth from him, Jesus turned about in the crowd and said, "Who touched my clothes?" 31 And his disciples said to him, "You see the crowd pressing in on you; how can you say, 'Who touched me?'" 32 He looked all around to see who had done it. 33 But the woman, knowing what had happened to her, came in fear and trembling, fell down before him, and told him the whole truth. 34 He said to her, "Daughter, your faith has made you well; go in peace, and be healed of your disease."**

Meanwhile, Jairus is getting desperate. It may be too late! In fact a messenger from his home rushes in to tell him that his daughter has died. Notice how Jesus now focuses his attention on Jairus to encourage his faith.

> **35 While he was still speaking, some people came from the leader's house to say, "Your daughter is dead. Why trouble the teacher any further?" 36 But overhearing what they said, Jesus said to the leader of the synagogue, "Do not fear, only believe." 37 He allowed no one to follow him except Peter, James and John, the brother of James. 38 When they came to the house of the leader of the synagogue, he saw a commotion, people weeping and wailing loudly. 39 When he had entered, he said to them, "Why do you make a commotion and weep? The child is not dead but sleeping." 40 And they laughed at him. Then he put them all outside, and took the child's father and mother and those who were with him, and went in where the child was. 41 He took her by the hand and said to her, "Talitha cum," which means, "Little girl, get up!" 42 And immediately the girl got up and began to walk about (she was twelve years of age). At this they**

> **were overcome with amazement. 43 He strictly ordered them that no on should know this, and told them to give her something to eat.**

When they reach Jarius' home, the yard and rooms are already full of people mourning this precious child's death. They laugh at Jesus when he tells them, "'The girl is only sleeping." Jesus once again isolates Jairus, his wife, and the three disciples from the disbelieving crowd. They enter the room where the child lies. Jesus takes this twelve-year-old firmly by the hand and says to her, "*Talitha cum*," which is Aramaic for "Little lamb, arise." The parents are overcome with great joy, with ecstasy, *ekstasei*, a word to be used only one other time in Mark, at 16:8, when the women are told that Jesus has been raised from the dead.

Notice how, jumping back a bit earlier in this story to when Jesus allowed only three disciples to join the rush toward Jarius' home, Jesus juxtaposed fear with trust. Jesus commands Jairus to trust, to cast fear off. "Fear not!" he commands, using the verb *phobeo*. In contrast, the verb usually translated "believe," *pisteuo*, predominates in qualities of faith rather than intellectual propositional affirmations about the world. It means to have faith, to trust, to believe in. "Have you no faith?" Jesus asked the disciples in the storm, using the corresponding noun, *pistis* (4:40) also juxtaposed there with fear. Using the same noun Jesus has just affirmed the woman who touched his robe in positive terms, "Daughter, your trust has made you well."

Three times in this chapter someone has fallen at Jesus' feet in desperate straits. Each time Jesus reached out in gentleness. "Daughter!" "Little lamb!" Friend! Rise up and be whole. Know *shalom*. But each occasion brings subtle nuances. It is, perhaps, no accident that these stories about faith come immediately after the disciples were chided for their lack.

The demoniac came to Jesus with some fear of the abuse he had suffered at the hands of others or perhaps fear of giving up his demons. Why did he run toward Jesus yet cry out lest he be tormented? A conflict pulls him both ways. Jesus surprises him, cleanses his spirit, and gives him himself. The woman indeed had trust in Jesus' power to heal her but feared making herself known. Yet if she did not grasp the opportune moment, when might she see him again? In the crowd no one would know the difference. She touched the hem of his garment from behind. Jairus came to Jesus trusting Jesus' power to heal another person, his beloved daughter. He humbles himself publicly to plead for her life. Along the way they are

"Follow Me."

delayed by a person from whom he would usually turn away. The news from home is bad. Jesus seems to run with Jairus, holding his faith in his hands, protecting him from the unbelieving crowds until they enter the child's room almost alone. Given these glimpses of their stories we find that, even for these who were helped and healed, faith is born in struggle.

Notice too how Jesus sticks with each person until his work with them is completed. The demoniac was a social outcast. Jesus stays at his side until the community gathers around and finds him healed, with a story to tell. Jesus sends him back to his former home to do what will not always be an easy task. Jesus starts out with Jairus and is interrupted. Jesus stops and turns to focus on the work being done through him at that moment, a woman restored, and he brings that act full circle before going on. Ever mindful of Jairus' need, Jesus will not let him go until his daughter is dancing around the room.

Then he charges Jairus and his wife and his own three: he ordered them not to tell anyone about this incident but to give the girl something to eat. Why is it that no one should be told about this act of power? Why tell no one? How, with the crowd just outside the room, can this child brought back to life be kept a secret?

Mark Chapter 6

6 He left that place and came to his hometown, and his disciples followed him. 2 On the sabbath he began to teach in the synagogue, and many who heard him were astounded. They said, "Where did this man get all this? What is this wisdom that has been given to him? What deeds of power are being done by his hands! 3 Is not this the carpenter, the son of Mary and brother of James and Joses and Judas and Simon, and are not his sisters here with us?" And they took offense at him. 4 Then Jesus said to them, "Prophets are not without honor, except in their hometown, and among their own kin, and in their own house." 5 And he could do no deed of power there, except that he laid his hands on a few sick people and cured them. 6 And he was amazed at their unbelief.

JESUS RETURNS TO NAZARETH with his disciples. On Sabbath he stands in the synagogue to share the good news. Many present are astonished at his wisdom but the response to him is mixed. Some seem to want to explain his wisdom, his power to heal; after all, Jesus is one of their own. They know his family and know that Jesus has been a carpenter by trade. They know he has not been to Jerusalem for an extended period of learning. Perhaps some of Jesus' family or friends were stung by what they took as his offensive public put down last time he was home (Mark 3:21, 31–33). Hadn't Jesus belittled them? Now he wants to preach to them? There may be echoes of the question raised by the scribes from Jerusalem (3:22). Is Jesus trying to lead people away from the God of Israel?[1] Why does Jesus needlessly

---

1. An important question. See Deuteronomy 13.

"Follow Me."

alienate the religious leaders? Whatever the reasons, they took offense at him. The Greek verb used here is *skandalizo*. They were scandalized. They took offense. Jesus, our boy, talking to us this way! This is the first report of a gathering swept up by the mood of his challengers. Jesus reflects on this as he suggests that a prophet is honored by many except for his own kin and home. But in saying this he reflects on himself in analogues to a prophet, one instructed or inspired by God to do God's work, and subtly reaffirms the claim he made in his debate with the scribes (3:35).

Jesus could not work with power among them because of their unbelief! The word is *apistis*, a negation of the faith Jesus instructed Jairus to try to hold (5:36).[2] Their lack of trust hindered Jesus' ability to work for their good. What should we think of this? From the beginning, Jesus' message challenged listeners to trust in the good news he brings (a form of the verb *pisteuo* was used in 1:15). Note the power this gives us. There is an amazing respect for the human in this interplay. We will not be influenced for the good against our will. It is a freedom granted us along with all the vulnerabilities that freedom brings. Jairus could have been swayed by the disbelieving crowd. A certain reciprocity, which brings with it an amazing equalizing power, is required for a relationship with God to work as it should.

> **Then he went about among the villages teaching. 7 He called the twelve and began to send them out two by two, and gave them authority over the unclean spirits. 8 He ordered them to take nothing for their journey except a staff; no bread, no bag, no money in their belts; 9 but to wear sandals and not to put on two tunics. 10 He said to them, "Wherever you enter a house, stay there until you leave the place. 11 If any place will not welcome you and they refuse to hear you, as you leave, shake off the dust that is on your feet as a testimony against them." 12 So they went out and proclaimed that all should repent. 13 They cast out many demons, and anointed with oil many who were sick and cured them.**

Jesus continues teaching in other villages. He has confidence enough in his disciples to send them out, two and two, with the kind of authority he himself has been given: calling for repentance, casting out demons, healing the sick, sharing the good news. This is why he chose them, for this purpose

---

2. The prefix *a-* negates the following word, *pistis*.

he called them apart and named them apostles: to send them out doing the work God had given him. And they go out proclaiming the good news in his steps.

Notice the instructions with which Jesus sends them out. You are to go without supplies, no soap, no bread, no money belt, not even a change of clothes. You are to depend upon the hospitality of the house you first enter. You are not to move around to better your accommodations. Your service is not to be given for your own profit. Your status is that of a sojourner in the land. Give freely. A town may refuse to hear your good news (as Nazareth had). In that case leave, shake off the dust from your sandals as a witness against them. But do not retaliate.

> 14 King Herod heard of it, for Jesus' name had become known. Some were saying, "John the baptizer has been raised from the dead; and for this reason these powers are at work in him." 15 But others said, "It is Elijah." And others said, "It is a prophet, like one of the prophets of old." 16 But when Herod heard of it, he said, "John, whom I beheaded, has been raised."
>
> 17 For Herod himself had sent men who arrested John, bound him, and put him in prison on account of Herodias, his brother Philip's wife, because Herod had married her. 18 For John had been telling Herod, "It is not lawful for you to have your brother's wife." 19 And Herodias had a grudge against him, and wanted to kill him. But she could not, 20 for Herod feared John, knowing that he was a righteous and holy man, and he protected him. When he heard him, he was greatly perplexed; and yet he liked to listen to him. 21 But an opportunity came when Herod on his birthday gave a banquet for his courtiers and officers and for the leaders of Galilee. 22 When his daughter Herodias came in and danced, she pleased Herod and his guests; and the king said to the girl, "Ask me for whatever you wish, and I will give it." 23 And he solemnly swore to her, "Whatever you ask me, I will give you, even half of my kingdom." 24 She went out and said to her mother, "What should I ask for?" She replied, "The head of John the baptizer." 25 Immediately she rushed back to the king and requested, "I want you to give me at once the head of John the Baptist on a platter." 26 The king was deeply grieved; yet out of regard for his oaths and for the guests, he did not want to refuse her. 27 Immediately the king sent a soldier of the guard with orders to bring John's head. He went and beheaded him in the prison, 28 brought his head on a platter, and gave it to the girl. Then the girl gave it to her mother. 29

"Follow Me."

> **When his disciples heard about it, they came and took his body, and laid it in a tomb.**

This is the clearest glimpse we get of Herod Antipas in this Gospel, a man who wields the power to imprison and destroy a Jew who might seem a threat to him or his family. Herod's wife hates John. Although he holds John the Baptist in prison, Herod has a certain respect for him. Herod would sometimes go to listen to John knowing he would be tormented by what he heard. We now get the story of his daughter's sensuous dance that aroused Herod and the Galilee leaders gathered for his birthday party, and how John's head ended up on a platter. His disciples came to give John as honorable a burial as possible.

The shocking story about John's death makes it easy to overlook the fact that the disciples have had a successful, if exhausting, mission. They are running on adrenaline. They return to Jesus to give him their reports. They have done the Lord's work, they now expect the Lord's reward. But there is no rest here. People crowd around with such demands that there is not even time to eat. Jesus suggests that they go to a quiet place to rest.

> **30 The apostles gathered around Jesus, and told him all that they had done and taught. 31 He said to them, "Come away to a deserted place all by yourselves and rest a while." For many were coming and going, and they had no leisure even to eat. 32 And they went away in the boat to a deserted place by themselves. 33 Now many saw them going and recognized them, and they hurried there on foot from all the towns and arrived ahead of them. 34 As he went ashore, he saw a great crowd; and he had compassion for them, because they were like sheep without a shepherd; and he began to teach them many things. 35 When it grew late, his disciples came to him and said, "This is a deserted place, and the hour is now very late; 36 send them away so that they may go into the surrounding country and villages and buy something for themselves to eat." 37 But he answered them, "You give them something to eat." They said to him, "Are we to go and buy two hundred denarii worth of bread, and give it to them to eat?" 38 And he said to them, "How many loaves have you? Go and see." When they had found out, they said, "Five, and two fish." 39 Then he ordered them to get all the people to sit down in groups on the green grass. 40 So they sat down in groups of hundreds**

and of fifties. 41 Taking the five loaves and the two fish, he looked up to heaven, and blessed and broke the loaves, and gave them to his disciples to set before the people; and he divided the two fish among them all. 42 And all ate and were filled; 43 and they took up twelve baskets full of broken pieces and of the fish. 44 Those who had eaten the loaves numbered five thousand men.

This episode, the feeding of the five thousand, is told in all four Gospels. The disciples play an interesting role in this story. They arrive with Jesus by boat to a place that was supposed to offer them some quiet rest; but people anticipated where they would go, and a crowd has already gathered by the shore to meet them. We readily understand Jesus being moved by the crowd. He sees their desire to hear more of the good news he has to share. Jesus cannot send them away. He welcomes the opportunity to teach.[3]

The disciples, on the other hand, came here tuckered out. They were hoping for their own quiet time with the master. They hang around for some considerable time watching Jesus interact with the crowds and listening to him speak. The hours pass. It grows late. They are hungry. They see the practical needs of the crowd. Jesus is so deeply engaged with the people he doesn't seem to notice. The disciples get impatient to send the crowd away, consult among themselves, then gently urge (command!) the teacher,

"It's late afternoon. We are in a deserted place. Send the people home so they can eat in nearby villages before it gets too dark."

"You given them something to eat," Jesus answers.

The disciples are taken aback. "What? Are we to find a bakery and buy 200 denarii of bread to give them?" (A denarius is the usual day's wage for a laborer.)

"How many loaves do you have on hand?" Jesus asks. "Go. See."

This they do to appease the master. They look. They count. They feel vindicated. They come back with some self-justification to tell him. "Five loaves, and two fish." It is a meal enough for a handful of people.

"Have the people sit down in large groups on the grass," he tells them.

The disciples do so and are soon back.

In Palestine in those days, the teacher usually sat while the listeners stood around him. It may have been less formal on this hillside. But now the crowds sit on the grassy hill while Jesus stands before them as the host.

---

3. At this point in the text we may wish that Mark had given us more of the content of Jesus' teaching to the crowds. Matthew corrects this defect with the Sermon on the Mount (Matt 5:1—7:29), Luke with the Sermon on the Plain (Luke 6:17-49).

"Follow Me."

They watch him tilt his head back and look toward heaven. He lifted the loaves one by one, blessed (*eulogesen*) the loaves, broke them, and handed repeated portions to his disciples to distribute to the crowd. In a similar fashion he divided the two fish and gave them to his disciples to share with the crowd.

On this late evening by the Sea of Galilee, the people ate their fill and there was an abundance left over. When Jesus had the disciples gather the remainder, they collected twelve baskets (*kophinon*) of pieces of broken bread and of fish. The *kophinos* was a wicker basket used by Jews.

> **45 Immediately he made his disciples get into the boat and go on ahead to the other side, to Bethsaida, while he dismissed the crowd. 46 After saying farewell to them, he went up on the mountain to pray.**
> **47 When evening came, the boat was out on the sea, and he was alone on the land. 48 When he saw that they were straining at the oars against an adverse wind, he came towards them early in the morning, walking on the sea. He intended to pass them by. 49 But when they saw him walking on the sea, they thought it was a ghost and cried out; 50 for they all saw him and were terrified. But immediately he spoke to them and said, "Take heart, it is I; do not be afraid." 51 Then he got into the boat with them and the wind ceased. And they were utterly astounded, 52 for they did not understand about the loaves, but their hearts were hardened.**

The disciples were put out to sea first to get the people moving. They obey Jesus but here they go, sent away without Jesus' company. That has to be discouraging. *They* are the *intimate* group. They still want to recount details of their successful mission. Soon the disciples find themselves at sea and at the mercy of a strong wind. They must take down the sail. If they were tired before, it really hits them now. They row just to keep the bow of the boat headed at an angle into the wind to keep the boat from capsizing and to keep waves from washing over the gunnels. They take turns rowing. They are exhausted. This time Jesus is not in the stern of the boat to awaken.

Suddenly one sees a ghost hovering over the water. They all look to see and are terrified. But it is Jesus, who calls out, "Take heart. It is I. Do not be afraid!" He is walking on the sea. Jesus' call, "Take heart!" translates the verb *tharseite*, (to be of good cheer, to take courage or take comfort). With the phrase "It is I. Do not be afraid," Jesus completes the command, once again, that fear be cast out and replaced with courage and trust. He places himself verbally in the midst of the command, and then bodily in their midst as he gets into the boat. The winds die down.

Only now the disciples get the report that after Jesus dismissed the crowds, he had hiked alone up a mountain to pray, to be refreshed with God's breath, but had left them in the storm until nearly dawn (the fourth watch of the night). And he had planned to pass them by? They hardly know what to think. Mark comments on their astonishment, how they failed to understand about the loaves, and their hearts were hardened.

Why does Mark leave the disciples with some lingering fear, or at least without a grasp of what has taken place? There is a kind of tension developing between Jesus and his disciples. We are inclined to focus on Jesus dividing the loaves and fish. Mark's concern with acts of power, with feeding the five thousand, or with Jesus walking on the water, is not to explain them. The disciples do not understand the miracles in that sense any more than we do. Mark wants us to dig deeper for something about the meaning of the act of power involving the loaves in context of his Jesus narrative. What is the significance of the loaves that the disciples failed to understand? What makes it difficult for the disciples? Why isn't faith simple?

The narrative provides no rest for the disciples or for Jesus when they finally get to land. In fact they do not reach Bethsaida on the far side, but land again on the west side of the Sea of Galilee at Gennesaret. Immediately Jesus is recognized and pursued.

> **53 When they had crossed over, they came to land at Gennesaret and moored the boat. 54 When they got out of the boat, people at once recognized him, 55 and rushed about that whole region and began to bring the sick on mats to wherever they heard he was. 56 And wherever he went, into villages or cities or farms, they laid the sick in the marketplaces, and begged him that they might touch even the fringe of his cloak; and all who touched it were healed.**

Fringes? These are the *tzitzit*, the tassels of violet blue wool attached to each corner of an outer garment. It was commanded by Moses: "When you see it you will remember all the commandments of the Lord and do them, . . . and you shall be holy to your God" (Num 15:39–40). Even this little detail about his clothing can remind us how much Jesus was a practicing Jew.[4]

And everyone who touched a fringe was healed.

---

4. Levine, *Misunderstood Jew*, 23–24. Chapter 1, "Jesus and Judaism," is full of such reminders of how Jewish Jesus is in his understanding of Torah, in his teaching, and in his prayer.

Mark Chapter 7

WE HAVE NOT HAD Jesus in a direct confrontation with the Pharisees and scribes since chapter 3, when Jesus was accused of working with Satan's power. Now, at a point in Mark's story where hundreds follow or even pursue Jesus, when he seems to be moving across Galilee from one foiled retreat to another for a quiet time with his disciples, the Pharisees stop him with a question.

> **7 Now when the Pharisees and some of the scribes who had come from Jerusalem gathered around him, 2 they noticed that some of his disciples were eating with defiled hands, that is, without washing them. 3 (For the Pharisees, and all the Jews, do not eat unless they thoroughly wash their hands, thus observing the tradition of the elders; 4 and they do not eat anything from the market unless they wash it; and there are also many other traditions that they observe, the washing of cups, pots, and bronze kettles.) 5 So the Pharisees and the scribes asked him, "Why do your disciples not live according to the tradition of the elders, but eat with defiled hands?"**

In his parenthetical comment, Mark makes it quite clear that the issue we are dealing with involves the tradition of the elders, the oral interpretation of the books of Moses. Mark may expect that some of his readers will not be familiar with such practices. But in this controversy we must not forget that this is an important issue, that the observance of food practices, of circumcision and of the Sabbath are also essential social markers in defining a Jew, i.e., identifying a Jew as a Jew for themselves and before the world.

We are looking at kosher food regulations with a focus on how one must wash hands before eating. The tradition specifies that the hands are to be washed, washed up to elbow using a handful of water. With Jerusalem scribes present, the Pharisees' challenge is not just a friendly gesture. But the tone is friendlier than the synagogue encounter over the man with a withered hand. They engage Jesus in good Jewish dialogue about the Law. My guess is that they are feeling Jesus out. They know that some of his actions and words suggest a messianic claim and, indeed, challenge their tradition. The question is one way to test the depth of his objections.

Jesus answers with strong words that raise the intensity of the conflict from his side. He first levels a broad attack on the oral tradition as some Pharisees practice it, with a quote from Isaiah 29:13:

> **6 He said to them, "Isaiah prophesied rightly about you hypocrites, as it is written,**
>
> > **'This people honors me with their lips,**
> > **but their hearts are far from me;**
> > **7 in vain do they worship me,**
> > **teaching human precepts as doctrines.'**
>
> **8 You abandon the commandment of God and hold to human tradition."**
> **9 Then he said to them, "You have a fine way of rejecting the commandment of God in order to keep your tradition! 10 For Moses said, 'Honor your father and your mother'; and, 'Whoever speaks evil of father or mother must surely die'. 11 But you say that if anyone tells father or mother, 'Whatever support you might have had from me is Corban' (that is, an offering to God)— 12 then you no longer permit doing anything for a father or mother, 13 thus making void the word of God through your tradition that you have handed on. And you do many things like this."**

Jesus illustrates the point of his criticism by citing the practice of Corban, which draws the Jerusalem scribes into the issue. A person could dedicate his or her possessions as a gift to the temple (in Hebrew *Corban* means offering or gift). From that point on the donor was not to use those possessions to help other people. In one serious abuse of its intended purpose, Corban was used to get out of helping one's parents by an arrangement that maximized funds going to the temple treasury. This arrangement, as Jesus claims, breaks one of the Ten Commandments, "Honor your father and your mother" (Exod 20:12); and adds his paraphrase of a nearby commentary on it, "Whoever curses father or mother shall be put to death" (Exod 21:17).

"Follow Me."

Jesus' point is that the very rules designed to enforce the Law are sometimes used in a way that undermines the intent of the Law of Moses. So Jesus is not going to insist that his disciples follow the tradition of the elders.

> **14 Then he called the crowd again and said to them, "Listen to me, all of you, and understand: 15 there is nothing outside a person that by going in can defile, but the things that come out are what defile."**

Let's not forget the context of this saying: talking about the disciples washing their hands before eating, washing up to the elbows. Jesus contrasts this act of cleansing the surface of the body with a concern focused on what the psalmist calls "a clean heart and a right spirit within" (Ps 51:10). But he used the words "*nothing* outside a person," which suggests a broader interpretation. It is a significant issue that the disciples ought to, and do, double-check with Jesus. They too need to test the extent of Jesus' objections.

> **17 When he had left the crowd and entered the house, his disciples asked him about the parable. 18 He said to them, "Then do you also fail to understand? Do you not see that whatever goes into a person from outside cannot defile, 19 since it enters not the heart but the stomach, and goes out into the sewer?" (Thus he declared all foods clean.) 20 And he said, "It is what comes out of a person that defiles. 21 For it is from within, from the human heart, that evil intentions come: fornication, theft, murder, 22 adultery, avarice, wickedness, deceit, licentiousness, envy, slander, pride, folly. 23 All these evil things come from within, and they defile a person."**

Jesus explains that what comes from outside, the foods you eat and what you drink, go into the digestive track. Whether Jesus meant his teaching to extend so far as Mark's parenthetical remark suggests, remains controversial. Amy-Jill Levine claims that "Not only did Jesus keep kosher; all his immediate followers did as well."[1] And it is right to point out that Peter called non-kosher foods "unclean" after the resurrection, as we know from the story that taught Peter that he should include the gentile Cornelius among the faithful (Acts 10:9—11:18).

---

1. Levine, *Misunderstood Jew*, 24–26.

Mark Chapter 7

Jesus' primary lesson, however, is the deeper point that we are not to let human precepts stand in the way of the word of God. How easy it is to become rule-defined, legalistic, and imposing those values on others whether it be in the form of traditions of the elders, interpretations of Scripture, church doctrines, or social expectations. But it is also clear that Jesus does not throw everything to the wind and say that it does not matter what you do. The contrast Jesus draws is that of the evil you intend to do and act on; *that* is what defiles you. The conflict between good and evil runs through the human heart. He lists a number of sins that more or less correspond to the portion of the Ten Commandments dealing with human relationships with humans. But then he adds two that are not in the Decalogue: pride and folly. Even in the act of making a loose list of sins here, rather than quoting six commandments, Jesus avoids turning them into rigid rules. He wants us to see the commandments as God's instruction that we apply voluntarily to the many interfaces of our lives.

Jesus replies to the Pharisees' challenge with strong words but with an answer that remains within the bounds of Jewish dialogue about the Law and its practice. This answer marks Jesus as taking a stand outside some of the oral tradition of the Pharisees. Yet it makes clear that Jesus takes the teaching of the Ten Commandments and the prophets as the foundation for knowing God's will. We are to obey the commandments intelligently out of love for God and other humans, not because it is a set of rules to be followed legalistically.

> **24 From there he set out and went away to the region of Tyre. He entered a house and did not want anyone to know he was there. Yet he could not escape notice, 25 but a woman whose little daughter had an unclean spirit immediately heard about him, and she came and bowed down at his feet. 26 Now the woman was a Gentile, of Syrophoenician origin. She begged him to cast the demon out of her daughter. 27 He said to her, "Let the children be fed first, for it is not fair to take the children's food and throw it to the dogs." 28 But she answered him, "Sir, even the dogs under the table eat the children's crumbs." 29 Then he said to her, "For saying that, you may go—the demon has left your daughter." 30 So she went home, found the child lying on the bed, and the demon gone.**

"Follow Me."

Not wanting to attract notice in Tyre, a Phoenician port city, suggests that Jesus is here to get away for that retreat with his disciples. He wants time with them to rest and to instruct them. A Syrophoenician (Phoenicia was a Syrian province) woman dares to come to speak to a man, a stranger, a Jew, a teacher (she breaks each of these cultural barriers). Throwing herself at Jesus' feet, she pleads with Jesus to exorcize an evil spirit from her daughter.

Jesus does not want a parade of gentiles coming to the door. He answers her, alluding to the Jews, "Let the children be fed first," and completes the thought with the image of a table scene with dogs in the house; "for it is not fair to take the children's food and throw it to the dogs."

This image places the woman in a very negative light. It is an insult to imply she is a dog or that gentiles are dogs. But this woman can spar using the very image he gives her. She does not give up. Her daughter's health is at stake! She answers with respect, saying, "Sir, even the dogs under the table eat the children's crumbs."

Jesus replies to her, gently. "For this saying, go home content. The unclean spirit has come out of your daughter."

The woman came in great need. She is clever, persistent, and, most importantly, trusts that Jesus can heal her daughter. Jesus does not accompany her. When she gets home she finds her daughter lying calmly in bed with the evil spirit gone. This is a powerful healing at a distance. It is another healing of a gentile.

Jesus gets some time alone with his disciples. We encounter them next going back to Galilee but by a rather roundabout way. They go first through Sidon, which is on the coast of the Mediterranean north of Tyre, and then evidently cut across the foothills of the mountains of Lebanon to Dan or Caesarea Phillipi and travel south on a road east of the Jordan River. They come out on the east, the Decapolis side, of the Sea of Galilee.

> **31 Then he returned from the region of Tyre, and went by way of Sidon towards the Sea of Galilee, in the region of the Decapolis. 32 They brought him a deaf man who had an impediment in his speech; and they begged him to lay his hand on him. 33 He took him aside in private, away from the crowd, and put his fingers into his ears, and he spat and touched his tongue. 34 Then looking up to heaven, he sighed and said to him, "Ephphatha," that is, "Be Opened." 35 And immediately his ears were opened, his tongue was released, and he spoke plainly. 36 Then Jesus ordered them to tell no one; but the more he ordered them, the more**

zealously they proclaimed it. 37 They were astounded beyond measure, saying, "He has done everything well; he even makes the deaf to hear and the mute to speak."

The command "Ephphatha," is said in Aramaic. "Be opened." This deaf man can now hear and begins speaking clearly. Partly out of the need to find rest from the crowds in Galilee, Jesus has extended his mission of mercy and healing to gentiles. Time and again a person comes to Jesus with a need, and Jesus responds to their faith and effectively ministers to the person. But that old tension between Jesus' request for secrecy and the inborn desire to celebrate a healing continues to be sounded.

Mark Chapter 8

8 In those days when there was again a great crowd without anything to eat, he called his disciples and said to them, 2 "I have compassion for the crowd, because they have been with me now for three days and have nothing to eat. 3 If I send them away hungry to their homes, they will faint on the way—and some of them have come from a great distance." 4 His disciples replied, "How can one feed these people with bread here in the desert?" 5 He asked them, "How many loaves do you have?" They said, "Seven." 6 Then he ordered the crowd to sit down on the ground; and he took the seven loaves, and after giving thanks he broke them and gave them to his disciples to distribute; and they distributed them to the crowd. 7 They also had a few small fish; and after blessing them, he ordered that these too should be distributed. 8 They ate and were filled; and they took up the broken pieces left over, seven baskets full. 9 Now there were about four thousand people. And he sent them away. 10 And immediately he got into the boat with his disciples and went to the district of Dalmanutha.

WE COME NOW TO a second gathering of thousands whom Jesus feeds in an act of power with food that he has blessed. The crowd has come to learn from him, and Jesus teaches. This time the disciples don't request to send the people home. They listen to his teaching for three days. Jesus turns to his disciples and tells them he is deeply moved (the same verb was used in 6:34), but moved this time by the crowd's physical need for nourishment. "The people need food," he says. "They may faint."

"How can so many be fed in this wilderness?" the disciples reply.

Mark Chapter 8

"How many loaves do you have?" asks Jesus.

They are ready for this. They say, "Seven. And a few fish."

And with steps similar to the ones taken on the previous occasion, the crowd is invited to find a place to sit and the disciples distribute the bread and fish.

Note Jesus' blessing over these morsels. The verb used in his blessing of the loaves (8:6) is *eucharisteo*, to give thanks, from which we get the word "Eucharist." In chapter six Jesus looked up into heaven and praised God in blessing the loaves and fish (6:41). Here he does the same over the fish (8:7). The Greek verb used is *eulogeo*, to praise or to bless, from which we get the word "eulogy." Thus we find Jesus both praising God and giving God thanks as he blesses the food. The loaves and fish are broken and taken by the disciples to share with the people. We notice that once again those present eat their fill and there is food left over, seven baskets (*spuridas*) full. The *spuris* is a large flexible basket used for carrying provisions or storing grain. It is the kind of basket, Luke tells us, that Paul will later be lowered in to escape from gentile Damascus (Acts 9:25).

It is worth noting that in this middle section of his book, Mark tells us that many persons, multitudes in fact, have sought some encounter with Jesus. So many have come to be healed physically or to deal with some distress of spirit that the individuals disappear into the crowds. But the identifiable people that Mark brings to our attention help make Jesus' work more tangible for us. Man and woman, girl and boy: a deaf mute, a woman with a blood flow, a blind man, Jairus' daughter, the girl in Tyre, and, in the next chapter, a boy; many Jews as well as a few gentiles. These are individual lives that Jesus touched.

Back in the present scene, Jesus dismisses the crowd that has just been fed and sails in a boat with his disciples to the district of Dalmanutha (or Magdala or Mageda—there are variations in ancient Mark manuscripts). Some Pharisees show up.

> **11 The Pharisees came and began to argue with him, asking him for a sign from heaven, to test him. 12 And he sighed deeply in his spirit and said, "Why does this generation ask for a sign? Truly I tell you, no sign will be given to this generation." 13 And he left them, and getting into the boat again, he went across to the other side.**

"Follow Me."

The Pharisees demand a sign from heaven, some proof of his authority, to demonstrate that Jesus' acts and words come from God. "Show us your portfolio, Jesus."

We sometimes demand proof. Explain these acts of power to me and I will accept Mark's account. Prove to me that God exists and I will believe in your God. Jesus responds emphatically to the Pharisees. "Amen" (*amein*) is commonly used in Jewish Scripture, an adjective meaning "truly" or "surely." It is usually found at the end of a sentence or of a prayer. "So be it!" Jesus characteristically puts the "Amen" first. Like his "Listen!" in chapter 4 while telling his parables but given with added clout: "This is the truth!" This phrase will show up more frequently as the pace of Mark's record slows down going into the second half of the book. "Amen! *amein*! You will get no further proof!"

Is it wrong to ask for proof? What is there about the Pharisees' demand that Jesus cuts short? Jesus seems to leave them quickly and we find Jesus once again with the disciples in their boat. Jesus is talking with them about this interaction with the Pharisees but using images which like the images in his parables can leave one wondering what precisely he is telling us.

> **14 Now the disciples had forgotten to bring any bread; and they had only one loaf with them in the boat. 15 And he cautioned them, saying, "Watch out—beware of the yeast of the Pharisees and the yeast of Herod." 16 They said to one another, "It is because we have no bread." 17 And becoming aware of it, Jesus said to them, "Why are you talking about having no bread? Do you still not perceive or understand? Are your hearts hardened? 18 Do you have eyes, and fail to see? Do you have ears, and fail to hear? And do you not remember? 19 When I broke the five loaves for the five thousand, how many baskets full of broken pieces did you collect?" They said to him, "Twelve." 20 "And the seven for the four thousand, how many baskets full of broken pieces did you collect?" And they said to him, "Seven." 21 Then he said to them, "Do you not yet understand?"**

Some disciples are puzzled at Jesus' statement about the yeast of the Pharisees and Herod. They are not thinking in metaphors. Jesus treats their lack of comprehension as if their understanding were no better than that of the Pharisees. "Are your hearts hardened?" he asks. One again we find Jesus using perception language in contrast to action language to address responsibility for understanding the world we are given. We had a dose of this in his parabolic discourse ("listen," "pay attention," "look", 4:3, 12, 24). You have eyes to see, ears to hear, a mind to discern what is happening in your presence. Even memory is brought in. Jesus reviews the details of the two miraculous feedings, down even to the detail of the two different kinds of baskets (*kofinos* and *spuridas*) used in collecting the broken pieces left over on each occasion. The disciples readily remember the details.

"Do you not yet understand?"

The same question was raised in Mark 6:52 after the first feeding of a multitude, and about the parables in 4:13. What do the disciples need to understand? What is the yeast of the Pharisees and of Herod? The Pharisees and Herodians have eyes to see his acts of power, ears to hear his teachings, but refuse to acknowledge or accept this as a sign that God is at work in Jesus. Jesus implies that if they would simply remember . . . , that would be enough. The sign is already before them.

Jesus will push his disciples further on this issue a few verses hence.

22 They came to Bethsaida. Some people brought a blind man to him and begged him to touch him. 23 He took the blind man by the hand and led him out of the village; and when he had put saliva on his eyes and laid his hand on him, he asked him, "Can you see anything?" 24 And the man looked up and said, "I can see people, but they look like trees, walking." 25 Then Jesus laid his hands on his eyes again; and he looked intently and his sight was restored, and he saw everything clearly. 26 Then he sent him away to his home, saying, "Do not even go into the village."

This curious healing occurs in stages. At first the Bethsaida man gets only halfway to correct sight. Why is this healing more difficult than usual? Had the man come reluctantly, dragged by his friends, and not by his own faith? But Jesus will not stop halfway. He lays his hands on the man's eyes again until his clear sight is restored.

Whatever the reason, it is at least symbolic that this two-stage healing occurs at this location in Mark's story. We have just been puzzling over whether the disciples, or we the readers, know what it is we are supposed to know, see, and understand about this man Jesus, standing before our eyes. Perhaps we too see in a haze.

27 Jesus went on with his disciples to the villages of Caesarea Philippi; and on the way he asked his disciples, "Who

"Follow Me."

> do people say that I am?" 28 And they answered him, "John the Baptist; and others, Elijah; and still others, one of the prophets." 29 He asked them, "But who do you say that I am?" Peter answered him, "You are the Messiah." 30 And he sternly ordered them not to tell anyone about him.

Caesarea Philippi is a gentile city twenty-five miles north of the Sea of Galilee ruled by Herod Antipas's brother Philip. During the next few chapters we find Jesus with his disciples on the way, walking south to Jericho where they will turn west to go up to Jerusalem. The phrase "on the way" (*en tei hodo*) will be used three times in association with Jesus' teaching about what he must face in Jerusalem, and what it means to be God's Messiah (8:27, 31; 9:31, 33; 10:32–34). We are reminded that this path is to be the way of the Lord (1:3).

Jesus questions his disciples. This is a crucial episode, a turning point in Mark's story. It gives some indication of how far the disciples have come, what they have learned as they have followed Jesus. It gives some hint of how far the disciples still have to go.

"Who do people [*anthropoi*] say that I am?"

There has been a good deal of preparation for this question in Mark's text. Demoniacs have called him "Son of the most high God" (5:7) or "the holy one of God" (1:24). Jesus has called himself "the Son of Man" and claimed that he has authority to forgive sins (2:10) and that he is lord even of the Sabbath (2:28). The disciples have asked each other, "Who can this be?" (4:41). His friends and neighbors have said, "He is only a carpenter" (6:3). Herod and his court discussed it (6:14–16). Then Jesus pops the question each of us must answer.

"But who do you say that I am?"

Peter answers, "You are the Christ."

The Greek phrase here is simple and direct, *su ei ho Christos*.

You are the Messiah. You are God's Christ. Peter has heard, he has seen, he has remembered, he has put it together to understand that the kingdom of God is indeed at hand, that God's Spirit breathes through Jesus, that Jesus is doing God's work. And in the meals he shared with thousands Jesus has hosted a messianic banquet, twice!

You are the Christ. It is the point Mark made in the very first sentence of his book. It is the title Jesus will claim when questioned by the chief priest at his own trial (14:61–2) and for which he will be condemned to death as blasphemer.

Mark Chapter 8

Jesus certainly accepts Peter's answer as true.

Why does Jesus immediately and sternly command his disciples not to tell anyone this truth about him? This has got to be a crucial moment for some insight into the messianic secret. Jesus has silenced unclean spirits who claimed to know who he is (1:25; 3:11–12). Given his acts of power and the extraordinary claims Jesus has made about himself, many Jews must wonder whether Jesus is the Messiah. But Jesus has not proclaimed it. Now he sternly prohibits his disciples from broadcasting it. They are to avoid making the direct public claim that Jesus is the Messiah. Why not proclaim it openly if it is true? For starters, Jesus seems to have his own understanding about what God's anointed one is to do.

> **31 Then he began to teach them that the Son of Man must undergo great suffering, and be rejected by the elders, the chief priests, and the scribes, and be killed, and after three days rise again. 32 He said all this quite openly. And Peter took him aside and began to rebuke him. 33 But turning and looking at his disciples, he rebuked Peter and said, "Get behind me, Satan! For you are setting your mind not on divine things but on human things."**

Jesus foretells that he is to suffer and be rejected at the hands of the highest representatives of the religious leaders he has come in conflict with, that he will be killed and raised from the dead.

Jesus makes this teaching with the strong claim that these things must (*dei*) happen to him. The impersonal verb *dei* means it is necessary, it is binding on one, or one must, one ought. It is not that God desires his servants to suffer. It is not that God controls what his servant or any person will do. Rather, in following what Jesus understands his Heavenly Father's will to be, Jesus has acted in ways that seriously threaten to undermine the religious and social status quo. Jesus understands that the religious leaders, who possess the human power in this "adulterous and sinful generation" (8:38) within limits set by Rome, will sacrifice him rather than lose their control. Jesus knows that this suffering is inevitable, *dei*, for the one who pursues the will of God in the way he has undertaken. This is the first use of this verb in Mark. We will note its further occurrences.

Peter immediately and strongly protests the picture of suffering and death that Jesus has just described for the Messiah. Peter's harsh words to Jesus and Jesus' harsh reply are described using the same verb, *epitimao*, to mete out due measure, to rebuke, or to censure. Mark has used this verb

"Follow Me."

when Jesus rebuked a demon to cast it out (1:25), insisted that others not make his identity known (3:12), when Jesus calmed the winds (4:39), and for his stern command to his disciples not to proclaim him publicly as Messiah (8:30). There are now two rebukes in this intense exchange between Peter and the master.

Peter has just confessed that Jesus is the Christ. Peter naturally expects that Jesus, who has now for the first time accepted the title Messiah as his own, will do great and glorious things in Jerusalem that will benefit all Israel and culminate in victory over Rome. It is an appealing script to hope for. When suddenly Jesus turns this common expectation on its head, saying that he will be rejected and killed by the highest authorities in Jerusalem, it is unthinkable to Peter. You are the Messiah! You must not be going to suffer. You must not be going to your death. We need tangible victory. That would certainly be my preference.

But Jesus emphatically denounces that kind of thinking. "You think as man thinks and not as God thinks!" Jesus speaks to all the disciples and not to Peter only, saying, "Get behind me, Satan!" Surely Jesus does not mean that Peter is Satan. On the other hand, what Peter has in mind is a definite temptation to Jesus. It presents him a genuine choice. Jesus could have refused the task of Messiah; he could even now choose to be the commonly expected Messiah. His emphatic denunciation demonstrates that Jesus has consciously rejected the role of a conquering Davidic king. His action throughout Mark, his teaching, this clash with Peter, all reflect the servant Messiah Jesus hears the Father calling him to be. Jesus turns now to instruct us as clearly as he can that *he* will provide the example we are to follow.

This is Mark's sixth and last mention of Satan, the fifth time the name occurs on Jesus' lips (1:13; 3:23, 23; 3:26; 4:15; 8:33). How does this use qualify the meaning of the term? Jesus took what Peter said personally. And it is not unlike the way Jesus spoke before: "How can Satan cast out Satan? If Satan has risen up against himself . . . his end has come" (3:23, 26). The one who "immediately comes and takes away the word" sown on the path was called Satan (4:15). To be consistent with this, Mark's "tempted by Satan" in 1:13 must mean at least that in the wilderness Jesus faced something like an encounter with one who, as Peter did, set before him an appealing alternative to the way God would have him walk.

Immediately after the rebuke Jesus begins to teach his disciples, both the twelve and the crowd of people with him, that his path is not going to be the easy or expected course. He teaches using the invitation, once again, to follow him.

> **34 He called the crowd with his disciples, and said to them, "If any want to become my followers, let them deny themselves and take up their cross and follow me. 35 For those who want to save their life will lose it, and those who lose their life for my sake, and for the sake of the gospel, will save it. 36 For what will it profit them to gain the whole world and forfeit their life? 37 Indeed, what can they give in return for their life? 38 Those who are ashamed of me and of my words in this adulterous and sinful generation, of them the Son of Man will also be ashamed when he comes in the glory of his Father with the holy angels." 9 1 And he said to them, "Truly I tell you, there are some standing here who will not taste death until they see that the kingdom of God has come with power."**

Jesus' original invitation to Peter at the seaside was open-ended. It can mean something as simple as, "Follow me, listen, come see what I do." And we have followed Jesus in this first sense in studying Mark, hearing his parables, observing though not necessarily understanding his acts of power. We saw the invitation take on more depth about the time the twelve were chosen and sent out ministering in Jesus' name. There it becomes something like, "Walk beside me, be my disciple." By the end of chapter 8 the disciples have come to the point of more precisely identifying who this Jesus is they are following. At this point in Mark, Jesus' words of invitation suddenly take a more demanding meaning. "If you would, indeed, follow me..."

Once again we face the problem of translating the Greek generic use of "man" and corresponding male pronouns into contemporary English. The direct translation of the Greek, "What can a man offer in return for his life?" (8:37, JB) for instance, is meant for women and children as well. The NRSV translation using "them," or "they," or "those who," or "their life," seems rather impersonal for the point that Jesus is making. One way to keep the question focused on the individual whom Jesus is inviting to follow him even here, whatever the person's sex or age, is to translate this passage as a direct address to the recipient.

"If any one of you would follow me, you must deny yourself, take up your cross and follow me. For, whoever you be, if you want to save your life

"Follow Me."

you will lose it. And if you lose your life for my sake and for the sake of the gospel you will save it. For what will it profit you to gain the whole world if you forfeit your life? Indeed, what can you give in return for your life? If you are ashamed of me and of my words in this adulterous and sinful generation, the Son of Man will also be ashamed of you when he comes in the glory of his Father with the holy angels. Amen, Amen I say to you, some of you standing here will not taste death before you see the kingdom of God come with power."

Jesus pursues the matter in the same sharp terms he used in rebuking Peter. The contrast lies between serving God and serving oneself. We sense the intensity of Jesus' commitment to God and God's kingdom. "If you would indeed follow me . . . ." And he employs an image every Jew must dread. The Roman Empire used the cross to execute dissidents. Rebels and insurgents were stripped, nailed to a cross, and given a slow, painful, and humiliating public death. Jesus need not have known that he would die on a cross to have used this image. Jesus might have expected death by stoning at the hands of the leading Jews in Jerusalem.[1]

And with a series of questions whose simple eloquence is unsurpassed in all of literature, Jesus spells out the contrast. Life is a gift. What will you give in return? Will you try to save your life in ways humans admire, gleaning power and glory or such wealth as to encompass the entire globe, and lose your soul in doing so? Will you give your life away in obedience to a loving God and discover you have found life? Jesus affirms that some persons standing around him will choose the path of sacrifice and experience the kingdom of God in its power.

We must note again how open-ended and how freeing the invitation "Follow me" is, even here. Jesus does not say, "You are mine therefore you must go do this or that." The invitation is strikingly unlike a military drill or a promissory commitment to march to the death. His way emphatically refuses to compel, to use force, to kill, to power over opponents or disciples. He may show us a need but he leaves the application to us. The invitation to follow remains open-ended; it frees us, but, of course, the burden of the content of his invitation is filled by the details of his own example. Could there be a loftier moral demand upon us? If you would be my disciple . . .

"If you would, indeed, follow me," he tells us, "I go before you."

---

1. At this point in Mark, Jesus has only predicted that he will die and rise again (8:31). Death by stoning was Moses' prescribed punishment for a person who blasphemes the name of God (Lev 24:16). Blasphemy has been an issue associated with Jesus' teaching (Mark 2:7; 3:28–29). Jesus will be tried and condemned for blasphemy (14:64).

Mark Chapter 8

Can we say more about the messianic secret at this point? Why has Jesus persistently inhibited the public proclamation that he is the Messiah? A good portion of the reason must involve the discrepancy between Jesus' understanding of how he is to carry out his task and the common understanding of what the Messiah would do. There are several ramifications of this point. In the first place, how are the followers of Jesus going to be able to see, to hear, to understand what his way involves if we are so blinded by our own contrary expectations? It may take nothing less than a strong shake, a rebuke by the master himself, to wake us up. "You think not as God thinks about these things!" Jesus still needs time to instruct and to show us the way.

A second point is closely related to this. Jesus has needed and continues to need to be able to walk freely in the path he understands to be God's will for his life. He needs to preserve his freedom to be the anointed Son, to proclaim the invitation of repentance into God's kingdom, to heal, to forgive, to instruct, to pronounce judgment where leaders miss the mark, to allow the power of God to be seen in and through his life, and to demonstrate what obedience to God may involve.

Third, and related to both of the above, Jesus could easily lose control of the focus were he to proclaim himself the Messiah too soon. Bands of zealots might immediately take up the sword against Rome and against the injustices around them without waiting for instructions. That outcome would obscure the clarity and courage required for Jesus' path. Jesus must control when he will make his claim public.

For disciples, what could be more central than this gem of information that he has now confirmed? Jesus is the Messiah! Isn't this Mark's secret of the kingdom of God given to disciples? (Mark 4:11). What more need he teach us? Our task, if we choose to follow, is to learn his way with him and to diligently explore how to walk that path in our own lives. There are dangers in the freedom this grants us. Perhaps Judas's temptation will be, in part, to force Jesus' hand as Davidic king? Can the insider's affirmation that Jesus is the Christ begin to corrupt the rest of us even as we walk toward Jerusalem?

Mark Chapter 9

IF WE HAVE LONGED for more of Jesus' teaching, we now find ourselves walking on the road with his disciples. It gives us a chance to learn in a different way than by extrapolating from Jesus' deeds.

> **2 Six days later, Jesus took with him Peter and James and John, and led them up a high mountain apart, by themselves. And he was transfigured before them, 3 and his clothes became dazzling white, such as no one on earth could bleach them. 4 And there appeared to them Elijah with Moses, who were talking with Jesus. 5 Then Peter said to Jesus, "Rabbi, it is good for us to be here; let us make three dwellings, one for you, one for Moses, and one for Elijah." 6 He did not know what to say, for they were terrified. 7 Then a cloud overshadowed them, and from the cloud there came a voice, "This is my Son, the Beloved; listen to him!" 8 Suddenly when they looked around, they saw no one with them any more, but only Jesus.**

With a specific time reference that Peter may well have told Mark, this episode takes place six days after Peter's claim that Jesus is the Christ. Peter, James, and John seem to be particularly close to Jesus among the disciples. They came with him when he healed Jairus' daughter. They now hike up a mountain with Jesus, perhaps Galilee's Mount Tabor or a foothill of Mount Hermon. Hermon stands north of Caesarea Philippi with peaks at about 9,100 feet above sea level that would be covered with snow much of the year. It is visible in the distance from upper Galilee.

    On the mountain Jesus is transfigured before them. Note that just two verses before this episode in Mark's text, Jesus spoke of coming in his Father's glory with angels. Our impression there was that he spoke of a return in the distant future. The experience on this mountaintop, however, is certainly one of Jesus in the Father's glory. Jesus is changed visibly before the disciples. He is transfigured; his outer garment shines with an exceedingly bright white light. It is a moment of radiant glory.

Two messengers show up. They talk long enough with Jesus for the disciples to identify them as Moses and Elijah, two great men out of Jewish Scripture who represent the Law and the prophets.[1] Both of these leaders experienced God on Mount Sinai at a moment when their task seemed most disheartening. Moses led his people out of Egypt to Sinai and ascended the mountain to receive God's instruction. On his descent Moses found the people worshipping the golden calf and in anger broke the tablets of the Law. Moses interceded for the people of Israel, climbed the mountain a second time, and saw the glory of God. New tablets of the Law were inscribed for the people (Exod 32:15–19; 34:1–5, 27–29). Elijah, the first major prophet, after fire consumed his sacrifice on the altar to demonstrate that the Lord is God, had 300 of Queen Jezebel's priests of Baal killed and then fled for his life. At Sinai he heard God speak in a still, small voice that sent him back into the struggle (1 Kgs 18:36–40; 19:3–18). All three men present, lawgiver, prophet, and Messiah, struggle with a people who find it difficult to keep God first in their lives and worship.

Peter can hardly constrain himself. He interrupts the scene, exclaiming at the marvel of it, to suggest that three booths be built to commemorate this exceptional encounter. We get the retrospective detail that Peter was so scared that he hardly knew what to say.

Another amazing thing happens. A cloud comes over them and from the cloud a voice: "This is my Son, the Beloved. Listen to him!" Does the voice chide Peter? "Stop talking. Listen!" But the message is more significant than that. In words that echo the affirmation Jesus experienced at his baptism, these disciples hear in third person, "This is my Son, the Beloved." These words provide meaning for the entire episode. Jesus is affirmed as being a part of God's long-term plan for the Jews, on a footing with Elijah and Moses; he radiates some of God's glory; and he is called the beloved Son in their hearing. The voice thus affirms what Jesus is doing and the path that he is walking. It affirms Peter's confession that Jesus is the Messiah. It commands Peter and those with him to be open to Jesus' instruction.

---

1. Luke tells us that Moses and Elijah were talking to Jesus about the departure he was to accomplish in Jerusalem (Luke 9:31).

"Follow Me."

> **9 As they were coming down the mountain, he ordered them to tell no one about what they had seen, until after the Son of Man had risen from the dead. 10 So they kept the matter to themselves, questioning what this rising from the dead could mean. 11 Then they asked him, "Why do the scribes say that Elijah must come first?" 12 He said to them, "Elijah is indeed coming first to restore all things. How then is it written about the Son of Man, that he is to go through many sufferings and be treated with contempt? 13 But I tell you that Elijah has come, and they did to him whatever they pleased, as it is written about him."**

The three disciples are instructed to tell no one about what they have just witnessed until the Son of Man be raised from the dead. They puzzle over what it could mean for Jesus to rise from the dead, even though they may be the disciples best situated to understand it. They witnessed Jairus' daughter raised up (5:37–42) and they have just witnessed Moses and Elijah alive, talking with Jesus. But the end of Mark will come before they understand it.

As they continue down the mountain, it occurs to them. Hey. Elijah was just standing there with you. The familiar prophecy in Malachi 4:5 comes to mind: "I will send you the prophet Elijah before the great and terrible day of the Lord." So they ask him, "Why do the scribes say that Elijah must (*dei*) come first?" Does this mean, Jesus, that God's day of judgment has arrived? The disciples' question tries to evoke an account of what is happening, or at least to clarify the timing.

Jesus gives them less than they ask for but plenty to think about. "Elijah is indeed coming first to restore all things," he answers, which puts an emphasis on Elijah's task from the next verse (Mal 4:6), with God speaking: "He will turn the hearts of parents to their children and the hearts of children to their parents, so that I will not come and strike the land with a curse." Elijah is to come with a call to repentance and reconciliation.

Jesus continues with a question. "How then is it written about the Son of Man, that he is to go through many sufferings and be treated with contempt?" And with a clear allusion to John the Baptist he adds, "But I tell you that Elijah has come, and they did to him whatever they pleased, as it is written about him."

Note that with "Elijah has come," Jesus directly implies that God's plan is even now being worked out, that both his own suffering and John the Baptist's suffering are part of that larger plan already put down in Scripture.

We may not hear what specific passages he is thinking of but Jesus affirms that it is there in writing.

The three disciples keep these matters to themselves for now. To put this in terms of the parable of the sower, there is a hint here in Mark 9:9-10 that the seed is in good soil even while the disciples fail to understand. One can follow Jesus without understanding many things.

When the four come down from the mountain they find the other disciples in some consternation. A man has brought his son to them for healing and they could not heal him. The man turns upon Jesus accusing the disciples. It presents a rather intricately woven situation we will view as a whole and then come back to note details.

> **14 When they came to the disciples, they saw a great crowd around them, and some scribes arguing with them. 15 When the whole crowd saw him, they were immediately overcome with awe, and they ran forward to greet him. 16 He asked them, "What are you arguing about with them?" 17 Someone from the crowd answered him, "Teacher, I brought you my son; he has a spirit that makes him unable to speak; 18 and whenever it seizes him, it dashes him down; and he foams and grinds his teeth and becomes rigid; and I asked your disciples to cast it out, but they could not do so." 19 He answered them, "You faithless generation, how much longer must I be among you? How much longer must I put up with you? Bring him to me." 20 And they brought the boy to him. When the spirit saw him, immediately it convulsed the boy, and he fell on the ground and rolled about, foaming at the mouth. 21 Jesus asked the father, "How long has this been happening to him?" And he said, "From childhood. 22 It has often cast him into the fire and into the water, to destroy him; but if you are able to do anything, have pity on us and help us." 23 Jesus said to him, "If you are able!—All things can be done for the one who believes." 24 Immediately the father of the child cried out, "I believe; help my unbelief!" 25 When Jesus saw that a crowd came running together, he rebuked the unclean spirit, saying to it, "You spirit that keeps this boy from speaking and hearing, I command you, come out of him, and never enter him again!" 26 After crying out and convulsing him terribly, it came out, and the boy was like a corpse, so that most**

> of them said, "He is dead." 27 But Jesus took him by the hand and lifted him up, and he was able to stand. 28 When he had entered the house, his disciples asked him privately, "Why could we not cast it out?" 29 He said to them, "This kind can come out only through prayer."

Jesus' first response, once he has heard the problem and his disciples' failure, is to cry out, "You faithless (*apistos*) generation." He bemoans the fact that he will not be around much longer to teach and be of direct help. The father who cried out to tell Jesus the problem had come in hope that he could get help. It seems now that nothing can save his son. Jesus calls for the boy. The boy is brought to him. The boy immediately falls down and rolls about in convulsions. The father explains that the spirit that convulses his son makes him unable to speak and hear. The boy has had this problem from a very young age. The convulsions sometimes happen near a fire or other dangers.

"Have pity on us. Do anything if you are able!" is the father's plaintive, desperate plea.

"If you are able!" Jesus chides the father for the doubt. "All things can be done for the one who trusts."

"I trust (*pisteuo*)!" the father immediately cries back. "Help my lack of trust (*apistia*)!"

Jesus rebukes the spirit, addressing its power over the boy's speech and hearing with a direct command, "Come out of him and never enter him again!"

With a cry and a terrible convulsion, the boy comes to lie motionless and limp. "He is dead," onlookers comment.

And with the same verbs (in the Greek) as those Mark used in the story of Jairus' daughter (5:41), Jesus firmly gripped the boy's hand to waken him and raised him up,[2] and he was able to stand.

How wonderfully human this father is. His own doubt had risen when it seemed that the disciples could not help. The disciples and those who had stood near enough to witness the scene came in doubt as well. Jesus addresses the father's doubt. The father responds, asking for help in trusting that Jesus can heal his son. Note how quickly Jesus acts before too many witnesses can gather adding to the doubt. The repeated uses of words related to the verb *pistis*, to trust, to believe, to have faith, in this passage remind us of Jairus (5:36), of the woman (5:34), and of the home crowd (6:6). In

---

2. My translation of this phrase.

each of these stories Jesus was surrounded by antagonistic, unbelieving, or even jeering people. As with Jairus, Jesus directs his effort into helping the child's father deepen his trust in God and acquire a confidence that can be strengthened, regardless of those around him.

When the disciples later ask Jesus why they could not heal the boy, Jesus answers, "This kind can come out only through prayer." No further clue is given here as to the kind of prayer Jesus has in mind. When Jesus next teaches his disciples about prayer (11:22–24) he ties prayer explicitly to belief, and to trust. And by his own example, when we next find Jesus in prayer, he is in Gethsemane earnestly conversing with his Abba in preparation for the difficulty, "the time of trial," that awaits him (14:32).

> **30 They went on from there and passed through Galilee. He did not want anyone to know it; 31 for he was teaching his disciples, saying to them, "The Son of Man is to be betrayed into human hands, and they will kill him, and three days after being killed he will rise again." 32 But they did not understand what he was saying and were afraid to ask him.**

This is a second round of instructions for the twelve disciples on the way to the cross. The next verse includes the phrase "on the way" (*en tei hodo*). With an emphasis on his betrayal and delivery into human hands, Jesus again foretells his approaching death and resurrection.

The disciples have been through this before. Last time, when Peter voiced the objection that things could not go that way, Peter got seriously chewed out. Jesus insisted that he must walk God's path and would not yield to Peter. Then, despite his error, Peter was one of three chosen to accompany Jesus to the mountaintop. The three came down all the more certain that Jesus is the Messiah. As Jesus teaches, again, that being the Messiah will soon involve his own suffering and death, it makes no more sense than it did the first time.

They are afraid to ask! We trust, at least, that they are listening.

> **33 Then they came to Capernaum; and when he was in the house he asked them, "What were you arguing about on the way?" 34 But they were silent, for on the way they had argued with one another who was the greatest. 35 He sat down, called the twelve, and said to them, "Whoever wants to be first must be last of all and servant of all." 36 Then he took a little child and put it among them; and taking it in**

> his arms, he said to them, 37 "Whoever welcomes one such child in my name welcomes me, and whoever welcomes me welcomes not me but the one who sent me."

This conflict comes right out of the new confidence that Jesus is the Messiah because, if he *is* the Messiah, *that* bears implications for his followers, particularly for the twelve. The dispute is over who is the greatest and, by default, who is the least. They try to consolidate their positions. After the second prediction of the passion! It is too human.

Jesus takes a little child standing in their midst, the smallest of the least, and in a gesture that occurs twice in Mark, he puts his arms around the child. At this moment Jesus makes explicit the theme of servant leadership embodied in his life and work. In his gentle embrace of this child, Jesus provides the model for serving in his community. The littlest child is advanced as a standard for the social structure of the community that would follow Jesus. To welcome a child means to receive the child graciously, to admit the child into fellowship, to accept the child as a person of worth. A leader is to serve the smallest person of all.

Addressing the matter of coveting the best place, Jesus tells them, "Whoever wants to be first must be last of all and servant (*diakonos*) of all." The *diakonos*, the deacon, is the person who waits upon, ministers to, and serves the needs of others. But this is not to be thought of as punishment, a despised obligation. This is not to be considered demeaning work among the followers of Jesus. For in serving the least child in Jesus' name you serve Jesus, and in serving Jesus you serve the Father who sent Jesus.

John jumps in with what looks like a distraction.

> 38 John said to him, "Teacher, we saw someone casting out demons in your name, and we tried to stop him, because he was not following us." 39 But Jesus said, "Do not stop him; for no one who does a deed of power in my name will be able soon afterward to speak evil of me. 40 Whoever is not against us is for us. 41 For truly I tell you, whoever gives you a cup of water to drink because you bear the name of Christ will by no means lose the reward."

The disciples, who have just recently had their own troubles casting out a demon, have taken it upon themselves to stop someone else from casting out demons in Jesus' name. Is John even listening to Jesus at the moment?

Jesus has just said, *"Whoever* welcomes a child in my name," which by implication, includes this non-disciple.

By a subtle hint Jesus also suggests that the disciples themselves will not always be the ones to serve but will sometimes be the least ones given help, and God in turn will bless that other person.

Jesus skillfully weaves John's question back into his own point about serving a child. He then expands the teaching to include a warning that disciples must maintain an awareness of their own lives and shortcomings. He teaches the lesson in a series of thoughts that flow one to the next by word connections.

> **42 "If any of you put a stumbling block before one of these little ones who believe in me, it would be better for you if a great millstone were hung around your neck and you were thrown into the sea. 43 If your hand causes you to stumble, cut it off; it is better for you to enter life maimed than to have two hands and to go to hell, to the unquenchable fire. 45 And if your foot causes you to stumble, cut it off; it is better for you to enter life lame than to have two feet and to be thrown into hell. 47 And if your eye causes you to stumble, tear it out; it is better for you to enter the kingdom of God with one eye than to have two eyes and be thrown into hell, 48 where their worm never dies and the fire is never quenched."**

We now hear the first of four comparative relations in which the first clause depends on the verb *skandalizo*, "to stumble," from which we get the English noun, scandal. The related noun is here translated "a stumbling block." Mark used the verb to describe the seed among rocks, persons who stumbled or fell away when persecution came (4:17), and for the group who took offense at the homebody in Nazareth (6:3). To put a snare in the way of a child, to lead a child into sin, to vex a child, to cause the littlest child to stumble, is a very serious offense in Jesus' eyes.

If Jesus' ministry began with a call to repentance, Jesus now teaches the community of his followers that they will not be perfect. The person sent to minister to others must look inward to face his or her own weaknesses and sin (7:20–23). We must not judge ourselves leniently but ("Repent!") turn dramatically away from the sin that binds us.

This set of images would likely catch the Jew off guard. In the purity code, a Jew who had a superficial blemish or was maimed was counted as unclean. Jesus teaches that it would be better to blemish yourself physically than to continue the inward invisible sin. On the other hand, we moderns are likely to be caught off guard by the judgment that fills the second half of the comparison. The word "hell" is the common translation for "Gehenna," the word used three times in the Greek text. Gehenna was a narrow valley skirting Jerusalem on the south that contained the city rubbish dump with its ongoing smoldering fire. In the first century, this Gehenna was used as a symbol for punishment after death, especially punishment by fire. Jesus teaches that sin brings punishment and death in its wake.

For the strong admonition to eschew sin embodied in these sayings, we must not miss the positive theme that flows through them. There is a choice. Throw sin away. Choose rather to enter life. Come in to the kingdom of God!

49 "For everyone will be salted with fire. 50 Salt is good; but if salt has lost its saltiness, how can you season it? Have salt in yourselves, and be at peace with one another."

Fire can purify metals, get rid of evil rubbish, and was sometimes used to cauterize a wound. Salt, as a less drastic measure, was put in wounds to purify them. Mark uses the nouns and cognates for "Gehenna," "salt," and "fire" only in this last section of chapter 9 (with one exception[3]). I will interpret them here as figures of cleansing or punishment. I suggest that Jesus is saying something like the following. We should do everything we can to avoid the cleansing fire that lasts forever. But everyone sins and must be cleansed. Salt, the less drastic cleanser than fire, works even in this life. Don't lose your salt, i.e., your sense of needing to be forgiven. Be willing to face your sin now and be healed. Be salty on yourselves and be at peace with one another.

This round of teaching begins with strife: disciples vying to be greater than the other and the conflict with an outsider doing good works. Jesus, in contrast, welcomes the stranger who does the work of peace and justice and mercy. Indeed, the disciple may expect to be sometimes on the receiving end of compassion. Disciples have no corner on a healing, redemptive ministry. The expected boundaries around the community of faith are simply not there. Jesus goes on to address the problem of scandal within the redemptive community. This chapter ends with his admonition to be at peace with each other.

---

3. "Fire" is used in its literal sense in Mark 9:22.

Mark Chapter 10

> 10 He left that place and went to the region of Judea and beyond the Jordan. And crowds again gathered around him; and, as was his custom, he again taught them. 2 Some Pharisees came, and to test him, they asked, "Is it lawful for a man to divorce his wife?"

THE WORD "AGAIN" REMINDS us of Jesus' earlier ministry in crowds and perhaps prepares us for the upcoming conflict. Pharisees are at hand. We last saw them when they accused the disciples of not properly cleaning their hands for a meal (7:5). The new question does not seem particularly hostile. The Pharisees ask Jesus about an issue that they debated heatedly among themselves.

Women did not have reciprocal rights under Jewish law at this time. The debated question was, on what grounds may a man divorce his wife? Moses permitted divorce "if she finds no favor in his eyes because he has found some indecency in her" (Deut 24:1, RSV). The house (school) of Shammai focused on "indecency" and argued that divorce should be granted only if the man had very strong grounds for divorce, such as his wife's adultery. The house of Hillel, on the other hand, allowed divorce for almost any reason, even if she spoiled a dish for him, by focusing on "some" grounds, in other words, "anything." Akiba will argue that divorce could be granted even if he found another maiden fairer, for it says "if she finds no favor in his eyes."[1]

---

1. The schools are described in this way in the Mishnah, *Gittin* 9:10, an early document of rabbinic Judaism. Hillel and Shammai were of the generation before Jesus. Akiba came several generations after Jesus. Danby, *Mishnah*, 321.

> 3 He answered them, "What did Moses command you?" 4 They said, "Moses allowed a man to write a certificate of dismissal and to divorce her." 5 But Jesus said to them, "Because of your hardness of heart he wrote this commandment for you. 6 But from the beginning of creation, 'God made them male and female.' 7 'For this reason a man shall leave his father and mother and be joined to his wife, 8 and the two shall become one flesh.' So they are no longer two, but one flesh. 9 Therefore what God has joined together, let no one separate."

In mentioning Moses, the Pharisees refer implicitly to the Deuteronomy 24 passage. In his answer Jesus quotes two verses from the creation story, Genesis 1:27 and 2:24. In Genesis 1, we find both male and female created in God's image. Genesis 2 focuses on male and female coming together as man and wife. Quoting the two verses from Genesis together in this way, however, Jesus brings out a lesson in God's will. Marriage is part of God's plan in creating us as sexual beings. God created us male and female for this reason (*hoste*): that the two shall become one in marriage. This union is of immeasurable value. Jesus concludes from this that "What therefore God has joined together, let no man put asunder" (RSV).

In this answer, then, Jesus focuses on God's will for the human male and female created in God's image rather than give permission for or prohibition of divorce. We should note that Jesus did not join the grand debate on the same terms as the question brought to him. He sided neither with Hillel nor Shammai. In this answer Jesus sets one Scripture against another, a portion of the Mosaic statute against the creation story. But, as always, his purpose is to seek out the will of God implicit in the text of Scripture and to put that to action. "Let no one separate what God has joined together."

The disciples, however, are not ready to let the matter drop. Jesus, is this a strict teaching against divorce? Won't you allow any divorce? Jesus answers again using strong words.

> 10 Then in the house the disciples asked him again about this matter. 11 He said to them, "Whoever divorces his wife and marries another commits adultery against her; 12 and if she divorces her husband and marries another, she commits adultery."

These words acknowledge that divorce occurs among humans and suggest that the person who divorces the partner and marries another continues to live with a certain hardness of heart. It is adultery. But we must carefully note that Jesus is not condemning any person here. That was the game he refused to be drawn into. Rather, he invites us to try to look at our lives from the perspective of God's will for us, and to live in that light.

Another important yet subtle difference from the question put to him by the Pharisees emerges in this elaboration. Jesus does not retreat from God's plan for humans as he speaks with his disciples but he maintains equal status in the eyes of God for the woman as for the man. As each was created in God's image and can marry, so each is given equal responsibility for the marriage. In context of Deuteronomy 24:1, given Jesus' teaching to the community of his disciples, the "least" in this concrete case is the woman. Jesus lifts her to a status of equality with her husband.

> **13 People were bringing little children to him in order that he might touch them; and the disciples spoke sternly to them. 14 But when Jesus saw this, he was indignant and said to them, "Let the little children come to me; do not stop them; for it is to such as these that the kingdom of God belongs. 15 Truly I tell you, whoever does not receive the kingdom of God as a little child will never enter it." 16 And he took them up in his arms, laid his hands on them, and blessed them.**

Jesus has repeatedly touched sick adults to heal them. Parents now bring their noisy children (merely!) to be blessed by Jesus' touch. Right in the middle of this serious dialogue, children come running. The disciples think it is not worth the master's time. They turn the children away.

Jesus scolds the disciples. He keeps the invitation open. "Let the little ones come to me." Then he takes them in his arms and blesses them. The verb for "he took them in his arms," *enagkalisamenos*, is used only twice in the New Testament, in Mark 9:36 and 10:16, the two verses in which Jesus takes children, the littlest people, and makes them the paradigm example and task for God's kingdom. Amen! he says; if we do not come like these children desiring to be blessed, we cannot even enter God's realm. And, from the earlier lesson a task: if we embrace a child warmly in Christ's name we welcome Jesus himself.

Jesus serves the children. Notice that the promise of the servant community which Jesus teaches (a new family, a community in which all

"Follow Me."

participants find acceptance, a place where the least is served first) is not enjoined as a command. Like Jesus' "Come, follow me" it is an open invitation: "Whoever welcomes one such child in my name welcomes me," and "Whoever does not receive the kingdom of God as a little child will not enter."

As we move on we continue to find Jesus teaching along the way. The teachings are spontaneous, when a disciple or a questioner provides the stimulus for instruction. Now a man comes in with the question, "What must I do to inherit eternal life?" The phrase "eternal life," is found twice in Mark, both times in association with this encounter. This man is coming to Jesus, a teacher who should know how to reply to this question. The man approaches Jesus, dramatically kneeling, flattering him with the title, "Good Teacher." Jesus refuses to play that game but immediately proceeds with the answer:

> **17 As he was setting out on a journey, a man ran up and knelt before him, and asked him, "Good teacher, what must I do to inherit eternal life?" 18 Jesus said to him, "Why do you call me good? No one is good but God alone. 19 You know the commandments: 'You shall not murder; You shall not commit adultery; You shall not steal; You shall not bear false witness; You shall not defraud; Honor your father and your mother.'" 20 He said to him, "Teacher, I have kept all these since my youth." 21 Jesus, looking at him, loved him and said, "You lack one thing; go, sell what you own, and give the money to the poor, and you will have treasure in heaven; then come, follow me." 22 When he heard this, he was shocked and went away grieving, for he had many possessions.**

When this man looks up at Jesus saying, "I have always done these things," Jesus looks into his earnest eyes and *loves* him. This is the only occasion in Mark where this verb is used directly to describe Jesus. Jesus feels a particular affection for this man. This is a striking note, particularly in view of what Jesus tells him out of this love. Your virtue puts you almost where you need to be. "You lack one thing."

Each of the commandments Jesus iterates apply to humans interacting with humans. But "do not defraud" does not, using that verb, appear in Moses' Decalogue.[2] The term "defraud" can refer to the act of keeping the

---

2. It does occur among the instructions of Leviticus 19 to "Be holy, for I the Lord your

wages of a hireling low (e.g. Mal 3:5). Does Jesus suspect that this man has acquired his wealth by taking advantage of others or at the expense of poor laborers, defrauding them? If so, Jesus gives him the task of making restitution. Is Jesus asking a rich man to enact the Jubilee moment in his life? The kingdom of God has economic repercussions in its wake. Does eternal life begin when you shift your trust from self to God? Jesus promises that *that* act, coupled with following him, will yield the treasure the man desires.

But note: we hear the invitation once again, "Follow me," now offered to the rich man. The pattern fits Jesus' call to the disciples from the security of their vocations to walk in his path. The pattern fits Jesus' instruction in 8:34–38 that if we really desire to follow him we must deny ourselves. And it most certainly fits Jesus' repeated instruction along the way, to serve the least person in our midst. But the full commitment implicit in the invitation hits this man as a sudden, unexpected blow. He was shocked! The man departed in gloom. Mark explains his emotion and response for us. His possessions, the Greek indicates, are landed properties. He owned many fields.

> **23 Then Jesus looked around and said to his disciples, "How hard it will be for those who have wealth to enter the kingdom of God!" 24 And the disciples were perplexed at these words. But Jesus said to them again, "Children, how hard it is to enter the kingdom of God! 25 It is easier for a camel to go through the eye of a needle than for someone who is rich to enter the kingdom of God." 26 They were greatly astounded and said to one another, "Then who can be saved?" 27 Jesus looked at them and said, "For mortals it is impossible, but not for God; for God all things are possible."**

We might be tempted to think that wealth, especially when someone has kept the Law as much as this man has, indicates that the owner is blessed by God and therefore stands well within the kingdom. But Jesus has warned how the lure of wealth and other worldly desires, or even the cares of this world, can choke out the kingdom (4:19). In the present context, the teaching seems to be that the more we have, the stronger hold that worldly infatuations and possessions have on us, and the more difficult it becomes to

---

God am holy" (Lev 19:2). "You shall not defraud your neighbor; you shall not steal; and you shall not keep for yourself the wages of a laborer until morning" (Lev 19:13).

"Follow Me."

rely solely on God. Or we get stuck on our merits. But not one of us can win the kingdom on our merits. The kingdom is God's freely given gift!

Notice how Peter so very nicely follows this up with an implication that comes right out of this scene before them.

> **28 Peter began to say to him, "Look, we have left everything and followed you." 29 Jesus said, "Truly I tell you, there is no one who has left house or brothers or sisters or mother or father or children or fields, for my sake and for the sake of the good news, 30 who will not receive a hundredfold now in this age—houses, brothers and sisters, mothers and children, and fields with persecutions—and in the age to come eternal life. 31 But many who are first will be last, and the last will be first."**

Jesus explicitly speaks about the present age and the age to come for the first time in Mark. The present age, *ha'olam haze*, will include ample rewards for the faithful (even fields), Jesus assures Peter, for those who sacrifice for the good news of God's kingdom, complete with the age's persecutions for the righteous. And in the age to come, *ha'olam haba*, eternal life is promised. This may mean life after death, but certainly it is an age lived in the presence of God, wherever and whenever that may be.

In his first round of teaching about his death along the way (*en tei hodo*, 8:27, 31), Jesus introduced the vocation of the cross as his messianic calling and invited disciples to follow his lead. It is an invitation to participate in sharing the good news of God's love in confrontation with the world. In the second round (9:31, 33) he invited his disciples to serve one another, to become a servant community. Jesus now speaks of his death a third time on the road (*en tei hodo*) amidst the uncertainty and fears of those around him.

> **32 They were on the road, going up to Jerusalem, and Jesus was walking ahead of them; they were amazed, and those who followed were afraid. He took the twelve aside again and began to tell them what was to happen to him, 33 saying, "See, we are going up to Jerusalem, and the Son of Man will be handed over to the chief priests and the scribes, and they will condemn him to death; then they will hand him over to the Gentiles; 34 they will mock him, and spit upon him, and flog him, and kill him; and after three days he will rise again."**

Mark Chapter 10

We find Jesus leading the way to Jerusalem. Those with him are fearful. Others seem to sense the disciples' mood and, guessing that Jesus faces dangers in Jerusalem, are amazed that Jesus walks with such confidence.

Jesus is not blind. He takes the twelve aside from the crowd and gives them the third and most explicit account of the suffering he foresees: someone will hand him over to the chief priests and scribes who will condemn him to death, and transfer him to gentile hands where he will be humiliated and meet his death. Gentiles are only now brought into the picture. Yet on the third day the Son of Man will be raised from the dead.

What Jesus teaches about how he intends to serve God in Jerusalem is difficult for the disciples to grasp. As if the tension involved in Jesus' instruction is too great for his disciples to deal with, the next episode, when two disciples can get Jesus to themselves, thrusts the messianic expectation in a radically different direction.

> **35 James and John, the sons of Zebedee, came forward to him and said to him, "Teacher, we want you to do for us whatever we ask of you." 36 And he said to them, "What is it you want me to do for you?" 37 And they said to him, "Grant us to sit, one at your right hand and one at your left, in your glory." 38 But Jesus said to them, "You do not know what you are asking. Are you able to drink the cup that I drink, or be baptized with the baptism that I am baptized with?" 39 They replied, "We are able." Then Jesus said to them, "The cup that I drink you will drink; and with the baptism with which I am baptized, you will be baptized; 40 but to sit at my right hand or at my left is not mine to grant, but it is for those for whom it has been prepared."**

Their request sounds like a phrase from our common prayers: "Do for us whatever we ask." Jesus does not play with that request. He responds to it at face value with the appropriate gesture, "Get specific."

The brothers get specific, and it brings us back to earth with what James and John are focusing on. They lay a claim to the positions of maximum recognition in the glory days they see on the horizon.

Jesus' next question, "Can you drink my cup or be baptized with my baptism?" encompasses the entirety of Jesus' ministry on earth. Jesus' baptism reaches back to Mark 1:9; his cup reaches ahead to the agony of 14:36. The verbs in 10:38 are in the present indicative. The question is: "Can you do what I am doing?"

"Follow Me."

"Sure!" They reply rather glibly. "We are able."

Note the gentle and discriminating response Jesus has for the two. "You will be granted the chance to drink of my cup and to be baptized with my baptism," Jesus assures them, not mentioning the absurdity and irony of their request when juxtaposed with Jesus' teaching on the way; and he assures James and John that they will bear fruit and that they will be faithful disciples. But the seating arrangement is left to God. By convention Jews use a passive phrase such as Jesus uses here to speak of God's action without saying God's holy name. God will grant the positions and distinctions in God's kingdom when the time is right. Jesus does not presume to make that decision. Indeed, the phrase "one on his right and one on his left" are used again in Mark's narrative but not to describe James and John.

> **41 When the ten heard this, they began to be angry with James and John. 42 So Jesus called them and said to them, "You know that among the Gentiles those whom they recognize as their rulers lord it over them, and their great ones are tyrants over them. 43 But it is not so among you; but whoever wishes to become great among you must be your servant, 44 and whoever wishes to be first among you must be slave of all. 45 For the Son of Man came not to be served but to serve, and to give his life a ransom for many."**

The other ten disciples are aroused to jealous anger. They are indignant that James and John should have attempted to short-circuit the road to glory. Jesus lays into all of them with a contrast that calls to mind the contrast he threw at Peter in chapter 8: you know the human way but you do not know God's way of doing things.

There may be a hint of irony when Jesus uses the verb *dokeo*, (to seem, or to be of the opinion that), in the phrase describing the gentile rulers. To put it literally, those "who seem to rule the nations" lord it over their subjects. "Their great ones are tyrants over them." But it is with a strikingly ironic present tense of the verb "to be" that Jesus addresses his disciples: "It is not so with you!" You are to minister to each other. "Whoever wishes to become great among you is to be your *diakonos*, your deacon." Mark uses the noun, *diakonos*, servant, twice in the master's emphatic teaching to his disciples (9:35; 10:43). Then, stressing this very point, "To reach the top, to become first of all, you must become everyone's slave," a *doulos*. This is Jesus' standard for leadership in his community. The kingdom of God is a serving community.

Mark Chapter 10

Why? Why is this God's way of overcoming the world? What does servant leadership accomplish? For starters, serving the other holds each recipient up as a person valued by the leader and by God. It is the way to express love and justice in an effective act. In that act, the giver shares his or her time, energy, emotion, and life. It is a leadership that frees the other person to be herself or himself; it does not try to control what the other person will do. Like a ransom, it frees the recipient. As foundation for this way of life, Jesus presents himself: "The Son of Man came not to be served but to serve and to give his life a ransom for many."

A ransom is an act that redeems or frees or delivers a person or thing from captivity or loss. The Hebrew verb *padha*, "to ransom," involves incurring a redemption cost such as paying money to compensate for an injury or loss (Exod 21:30), or making an offering to God that redeems a firstborn male child (Num 18:15-16). Another verb, *gaal*, "to redeem, to act as kinsman," provides a unique and purely Jewish flavor to this notion. The Hebrew word *goel* is the next of kin who acts to redeem property or purchase the freedom of a relative who has fallen on bad times (Lev 25:25). In a famous love story, Boaz redeems Ruth by purchasing a parcel of land that belonged to her mother-in-law, an act that also allows Boaz to marry Ruth (Ruth 4:3-6).

When Jesus says, "The Son of Man came to give his life as a ransom for many," we usually understand this claim in light of what Jesus tells us he faces in Jerusalem, that he plans to serve others by his death and through that act to redeem many persons from their sins. And we will watch him resolutely pursue that course. As I listen to him this time, however, I wonder if there may be an additional dimension to what Jesus is saying. Isn't Jesus consciously and intentionally living his life in a manner that repeatedly redeems others? His teaching, his words of encouragement, his healing acts of power, and giving of himself daily as he serves others, each of these actions is done in response to some personal need or suffering. His action is not done for self-acclaim. A certain cost is incurred in this kind of giving that frees the other in some way. It redeems. This too may be what it means to serve others as he serves.

> **46 They came to Jericho. As he and his disciples and a large crowd were leaving Jericho, Bartimaeus son of Timaeus, a blind beggar, was sitting by the roadside. 47 When he heard that it was Jesus of Nazareth, he began to shout out and say, "Jesus, Son of David, have mercy on me!" 48 Many sternly**

"Follow Me."

> ordered him to be quiet, but he cried out even more loudly, "Son of David, have mercy on me!" 49 Jesus stood still and said, "Call him here." And they called the blind man, saying to him, "Take heart; get up, he is calling you." 50 So throwing off his cloak, he sprang up and came to Jesus.

Jesus and those with him now turn west for the last leg of their journey. As Jericho sits at 800 feet below sea level (the Dead Sea lies more than 1,200 below) and Jerusalem at about 2,600 above sea level, they anticipate a fifteen-mile uphill hike. They hardly get started.

Beside the road sits a blind beggar, the son of Timaeus. Passover is bounty season for a beggar. Pilgrims have a little money to spare. No one wants to arrive in Jerusalem on this holy festival feeling selfish. Over the noise of the crowd and the shuffle of feet, Bartimaeus hears the name, Jesus. He makes out that Jesus, the man of Nazareth, is passing by in the multitude. He calls out to him, "Jesus, Son of David!" using a title that designates the royal Messiah. It is blind Bartimaeus who identifies him, who from the side of the road calls out, "Jesus, Messiah." Only the disciples (demons have come close) have addressed him this way before. Bartimaeus calls and is pushed back by the crowd. But he persists, loudly. He appeals personally to Jesus. Jesus cannot simply ignore him.

Once more Jesus turns to minister to a person others have pushed aside. He calls Bartimaeus. Bartimaeus's response is dramatic. He throws off the cloak that blind beggars spread on the ground to catch the coins that pilgrims toss their way, and walks toward the voice that says, "Come! I am here." And with the same words used in responding to James and John:

> 51 Then Jesus said to him, "What do you want me to do for you?" The blind man said to him, "My teacher, let me see again." 52 Jesus said to him. "Go. Your faith has made you well." Immediately he regained his sight and followed him on the way.

So, given new eyesight, Bartimaeus does not simply go home. He follows Jesus on the way (*en tei hodo*) to Jerusalem. He comes and he will see.

Mark Chapter 11

WE ARE NOW APPROACHING Jerusalem which, with nearby villages, will be the setting for the remainder of the book of Mark. In the first verses of chapter 1, we noted Mark's allusion to the prophet Malachi when he said, "See, I am sending my messenger to prepare the way before me" (Mal 3:1), which we found could apply to John the Baptist. The remainder of that verse is worth noting as we go forward. "And the Lord whom you seek will suddenly come to his temple. The messenger of the covenant in whom you delight—indeed, he is coming, says the Lord of hosts."

> 11 When they were approaching Jerusalem, at Bethphage and Bethany, near the Mount of Olives, he sent two of his disciples 2 and said to them, "Go into the village ahead of you, and immediately as you enter it, you will find tied there a colt that has never been ridden; untie it and bring it. 3 If anyone says to you, 'Why are you doing this?' just say this, 'The Lord needs it and will send it back here immediately.'" 4 They went away and found a colt tied near a door, outside in the street. As they were untying it, 5 some of the bystanders said to them, "What are you doing, untying the colt?" 6 They told them what Jesus had said; and they allowed them to take it.

Jesus gives two of his disciples these rather mysterious instructions on where to find a young colt and how to go about borrowing it. They follow his instructions and are allowed to take the colt. Jesus plans to enter Jerusalem on a colt! It is his conscious intention to do so.

The episode of Jesus' triumphal entry to Jerusalem poses a problem. Jesus carries out a well-defined messianic act expecting it to be so interpreted by the crowds of people around him.

"Follow Me."

What is the messianic act? There was a familiar prophecy in Zechariah that says:

> 9 Rejoice greatly, O daughter of Zion!
> Sing aloud, O daughter of Jerusalem!
> Lo, your king comes to you; triumphant and victorious is he,
> humble, and riding on a donkey, on a colt, the foal of a donkey.
> (Zech 9:9)

Zechariah 9 is a song of God's victory, with verses 1–8 enumerating the defeat of Israel's enemies. Verse 9 cries out, rejoicing for the triumphant king returning to Jerusalem to initiate a reign in Zion. In the remainder of chapter 9 God will empower the people of Zion and their king will rule with peace over all nations to the ends of the earth.

What is the problem? Since the beginning of his ministry Jesus has prevented the demon-spirited from proclaiming that he is the Messiah. At Peter's confession and again after the transfiguration, Jesus commanded his disciples to tell no one that he is the Messiah. In the last three chapters Jesus has been struggling to get his disciples to listen to him, to come to understand that he is not going to be the triumphant Messiah they expect, that he will not rule like an earthly king but will be killed and raised from the dead. Perhaps because of this very understanding of his task, Jesus has not claimed publicly that he is the Messiah. Why does Jesus now deliberately and openly enter Jerusalem as the expected Messiah? The crowds will understand what they see, that their king, the son of David, is entering Jerusalem to rule in triumph, precisely the vision Peter had in chapter 8. Why doesn't Jesus correct them? He allows them, even encourages them, to proclaim that vision about him on every side. What is Jesus doing?

> **7 Then they brought the colt to Jesus and threw their cloaks on it; and he sat on it. 8 Many people spread their cloaks on the road, and others spread leafy branches that they had cut in the fields. 9 Then those who went ahead and those who followed were shouting,**
>
> > "Hosanna!
> > Blessed is the one who comes in the name of the Lord!
> > 10 Blessed is the coming kingdom of our ancestor David!
> > Hosanna in the highest heaven!"

Let's not forget that Bartimaeus started something when he heard that Jesus was passing by. "Jesus, son of David, have mercy on me!" Bartimaeus was insistent. He would not let Jesus pass by without heeding him. Jesus gave his blind eyes sight and Bartimaeus followed him. The crowd had witnessed another act of power, but, more significantly, Jesus did not deny his Davidic descent. That fact has no doubt been repeated from mouth to mouth, circulating in this crowd throughout the ascent to Jerusalem. Aware of this, Jesus seeks out a colt to ride into the city. This crowd is ready the moment Jesus sits on the colt. The crowd's response is joyful and enthusiastic.

In 1994 I attended a portion of a study on the Jewish holidays in the book of Matthew for a small group of Christians led by Myron Kinberg, the rabbi of Temple Beth Israel in Eugene. We came to Matthew 21, which is a close parallel (with some additions) to Mark 11. As Rabbi Kinberg taught us, this chapter shows a dramatic change in the character of Jesus' action. This chapter sounds the theme of Jesus' authority. Jesus assumes the authority of Messiah.

The Songs of Ascents, Psalms 120–134, Rabbi Kinberg continued, were sung by pilgrims on their way up to Jerusalem. We looked at Psalm 118, the primary text of the Hallel, a focus of the prayer service on each of the high feast days.

> 25 Save us [*Hoshianna*], we beseech you, O Lord!
>
> O Lord, we beseech you, give us success!
>
> 26 Blessed is the one who comes in the name of the Lord.
>
> We bless you from the house of the Lord. (Ps 118:25–26)

For the ritual of the Lulab in the fall Festival of Booths, pilgrims come with a branch of myrtle or palm to be waved as the procession circles the altar. On the way to the temple on this particular spring day, pilgrims waved branches, threw their cloaks on the ground, and adapted the psalm in light of the colt Jesus was riding. Rabbi Kinberg read the text for us:

> 9 "*Hoshianna* [Hosanna] to the Son of David!
>
> Blessed is the one who comes in the name of the Lord!
>
> *Hoshianna* [Hosanna] in the highest heaven!" (Matt 21:9)

I asked Rabbi Kinberg, "Would the common people have recognized the ride on the ass as a messianic act?"

"Indeed they would," he answered. "They would be familiar with the prophetic passage. In fact this is confirmed by the text itself," he added, "in

"Follow Me."

which people coming to the high feast spread their cloaks on the ground before him, cut branches, and shouted, '*Hoshianna* to the Son of David!'" This procession may have continued its march, waving branches and cheering, into the courtyard of the temple itself.[1]

> **11 Then he entered Jerusalem and went into the temple; and when he had looked around at everything, as it was already late, he went out to Bethany with the twelve.**
> **12 On the following day, when they came from Bethany, he was hungry. 13 Seeing in the distance a fig tree in leaf, he went to see whether perhaps he would find anything on it. When he came to it, he found nothing but leaves, for it was not the season for figs. 14 He said to it, "May no one ever eat fruit from you again." And his disciples heard it.**

This is the second day in Jerusalem. Mark gives more details about time and place and names more persons who are not in Jesus' immediate group in the last six chapters than the first two-thirds of the book. The events occur within the frame of seven days.[2] The text makes some claims that can intersect with other historical records: that Jesus was crucified under Pontius Pilate as "King of the Jews."

The strange incident of the fig tree makes a bracket around the next incident. Jesus is hungry and has angry words for a fig tree with no figs. We'll take this up again at verse 20.

There was a wide courtyard around the temple, the Court of the Gentiles, that everyone, including foreigners, was allowed to enter. Foreigners could not go beyond a certain boundary. Inside that boundary and closer to the temple was the Woman's Court that all Jews could enter; and closer to the temple itself was the Court of Israel that was restricted for Jewish men.[3] Thousands of birds and unblemished animals that would be used for ritual

---

1. Rabbi Kinberg was sympathetic to many of the teachings of Jesus as he explained them to us. He avoided a direct answer to someone's question whether he believed Jesus to be the Messiah. This was entirely appropriate. I believe he subtly encouraged us not to make this an issue between us. A crucial feature of Rabbi Kinberg's work was to build bridges between the Jewish and Christian and Islamic communities in the US, and, from the stories I have heard, he repeatedly put his own life at risk in doing the same each time he visited Israel and Palestine. In this work and the manner in which he went about it, Rabbi Kinberg will forever have my deepest respect and admiration.

2. The days are implied in the passage of time in the following verses: 11:11; 11:12, 19; 11:20, 27, 13:1; 14:12, 17; 15:1, 33, 42; the sabbath; 16:1–2.

3. Stinespring, "Temple, Jerusalem," 556–57.

sacrifice in the temple during this Passover festival would be available for sale in the Court of the Gentiles.

> **15 Then they came to Jerusalem. And he entered the temple and began to drive out those who were selling and those who were buying in the temple, and he overturned the tables of the money changers and the seats of those who sold doves; 16 and he would not allow anyone to carry anything through the temple. 17 He was teaching and saying, "Is it not written,**
>
> > **'My house shall be called a house of prayer for all the nations'?**
> > **But you have made it a den of robbers."**
>
> **18 And when the chief priests and the scribes heard it, they kept looking for a way to kill him; for they were afraid of him, because the whole crowd was spellbound by his teaching. 19 And when evening came, Jesus and his disciples went out of the city.**

Why does Jesus drive the sellers and money changers out of the Court of the Gentiles? Foreigners were allowed to worship in this vicinity of the temple. One might expect that the commotion of the ongoing money exchange and trade for sacrificial animals would make it difficult for a person close by to worship. But more pointedly, "Let the temple return to its true purpose," Jesus cries, which is, quoting Isaiah 56:7, to be a joyful house of prayer for all peoples. "But you have made it a den of robbers," Jesus adds, with an allusion to Jeremiah, who asks "Do you take this Temple that bears my name for a robber's den?" (Jer 7:11, JB). Jeremiah goes on to answer his question in 7:14, "I will treat this Temple . . . just as I treated Shiloh" (JB). And to bring this thought full circle, in the days when Samuel was becoming the prophet in Israel, a Philistine army defeated the Israelites, destroyed the house of worship at Shiloh, and captured Israel's most sacred object, the ark of the covenant with God (1 Sam 4:10–11).

It would not be the first nor last time the accusation of robbery was leveled against the temple. Temple authorities determined which lambs could be sacrificed in the temple, provided the banking system, and set the exchange rate for the money that could be used to purchase sacrificial items. There were times when the price of doves, the only sacrifice that poor people were expected to afford, was unfairly high. There is evidence that shops in the temple area belonged to the high priestly family. Some rabbis charged that the temple was going to moral ruin because of greed and hatred. Josephus called the high priest Ananias (in office from 47–55 CE) "the great procurer of money."[4]

Whatever else Jesus' act may be, it is certainly a direct challenge to temple authority. If he entered Jerusalem as Messiah, here Jesus assumes a certain authority over the temple. He drives out persons who sell and buy sacrificial animals, and he overturns the tables and chairs involved in a practice approved by the chief priest. He pronounces a prophetic judgment against the temple. The entire act must take place in a rather short time. It did not disrupt or incite enough people to bring in the Roman soldiers who are at alert in Jerusalem during the Passover Festival, and ready to quell any disturbance with force.

The reaction of the temple leadership is strong but, at least at first, expressed primarily among themselves. They consult with one another about whether they can find a way to get rid of Jesus. In fact the temple administrators act with restraint. There is a very practical side to this problem. Temple power, given Roman control, depends on the control the high priests can exert over the crowds. Jesus has assumed the authority of a Messiah. He has directly challenged temple authority and is now teaching openly in the temple courtyard. The temple administrators must find the way to answer him lest he bring down their whole power-sharing arrangement with the Romans. Jesus is their problem. What is the solution?

That evening Jesus left the city of Jerusalem with his disciples. The narrative continues on the following day.

> **20 In the morning as they passed by, they saw the fig tree withered away to its roots. 21 Then Peter remembered and said to him, "Rabbi, look! The fig tree that you cursed has withered." 22 Jesus answered them, "Have faith in God. 23 Truly I tell you, if you say to this mountain, 'Be taken up and thrown into the sea,' and if you do not doubt in your heart, but believe that what you say will come to pass, it will be done for you. 24 So I tell you, whatever you ask for in prayer, believe that you have received it, and it will be yours.**
>
> **25 Whenever you stand praying, forgive, if you have anything against anyone; so that your Father in heaven may also forgive you your trespasses."**

---

4. Jeremias, *Jerusalem in the Time of Jesus*, 33–34, 48–49.

Jesus is not as surprised as Peter over the fact that his "curse" on the fig tree was effective. He immediately moves into a lesson about the power of prayer when it is based on a profound trust in God. The verb *pisteuo* (to trust, to have faith, to believe) is used three times in these verses.

What can we learn from Jesus' response? Jesus evidently treats his own angry words as a kind of prayer. As he lives this portion of his life in the presence of his Father Jesus seems to consider that everything he says and does becomes a kind of prayer. Two: Perhaps Jesus finds a suggestion in the fig tree. If this is what can happen to a fig tree that you address in anger, do not forget to control your temper. Keep your head in the week coming up. You will be threatened with stronger compulsions than with hunger. Three: Jesus draws some lessons on prayer for us. When you pray trusting that prayer is answered with the Father's power, do not be surprised when the prayer is answered with the Father's power. When you stand at prayer remember to forgive your enemies and forgive any person when there is something unforgiven between you. Do not curse them to their harm. Remember the One with the power to answer prayer. God has power over you and your life. Ask that your own sins be forgiven.

We should note, whether we stand in the temple or stand before the fig tree, that Jesus' prayer intersects with the utterly practical matters of daily life: hunger, the ability to afford the sacrifice, fruit-bearing trees, the exchange of money, a place near the temple to pray, anger, our constant presence before God. Trust in God is to include even such details of our lives.

The disciples continue their walk with Jesus into Jerusalem.

> **27 Again they came to Jerusalem. As he was walking in the temple, the chief priests, the scribes, and the elders came to him 28 and said, "By what authority are you doing these things? Who gave you this authority to do them?" 29 Jesus said to them, "I will ask you one question; answer me, and I will tell you by what authority I do these things. 30 Did the baptism of John come from heaven, or was it of human origin? Answer me." 31 They argued with one another, "If we say, 'From heaven,' he will say, 'Why then did you not believe him?' 32 But shall we say, 'Of human origin?'"—they were afraid of the crowd, for all regarded John as truly a prophet. 33 So they answered Jesus, "We do not know." And Jesus said to them, "Neither will I tell you by what authority I am doing these things."**

"Follow Me."

The chief priests, scribes, and elders walking together represent the core of temple power, probably the Sanhedrin itself, the supreme council of the Jews. They come as an identifiable group to address Jesus with a question. The focal issue concerns the authority that Jesus is openly assuming. "What authority do you have, Jesus? On whose authority do you act?"

I suspect the temple authorities want Jesus to make the outright claim that he is the Messiah acting with God's authority. Jesus has yet to demonstrate he is capable of being the expected king by raising revolt to free Israel from Roman oppression, one to conquer and demand tribute from all the nations. Hasn't he gone about matters in the wrong way? Hasn't he challenged the Law of Moses, our very heritage? Our Jerusalem authorities have warned him publicly that he is leading people astray (3:22). Now he challenges God's authority on temple grounds! How can he expect to get far without temple backing? Surely there are still enough people who will find him an imposter. They might arrest him if he proves false.

So they come probing. "What authority do you have, Jesus? On whose behalf do you act?" But Jesus returns their question to them with a challenge. "Answer me this question," he says, "then I will answer you. Was John the Baptist's work authorized by God or by man?"

Mark gives us a glimpse of the discussion of the temple authorities that ensues. Should we claim John's baptism was authorized by God? The people believe he was a prophet, but we did not believe him. But if we say his authority was only human the crowd will turn against us. "We do not know," they said to Jesus. This answer hints that, at least in Mark's perspective, the grounds for the leaders' own authority is human, subject to humans and fearful of humans.

Jesus then replies: "Neither will I tell you by what authority I am doing these things."

What would have been the answer to their question? Jesus did not act with the temple's authority. That was clear to everyone. We know, given the first sentence and verses of Mark, that Jesus could claim that his authority and John the Baptist's authority come from God. By juxtaposing his own position with that of John the Baptist in his response, Jesus answers the question without answering the question. Jesus has bypassed human authority over the temple. He does not fear the temple leadership.

Consider in summary the related question I raise, why did Jesus come into Jerusalem so openly as Messiah? Jesus comes to Jerusalem in obedience to what he understands to be God's will for his life. He understands that he is God's beloved son. He understands that his task is not to become the expected military Davidic king but to obey the Father's will even unto death in Jerusalem. He is God's Christ. But if he is to face death here, it will be done openly, as God's Messiah.

So Jesus seeks to do his Father's will in a given situation. At the start of the ascent to Jerusalem, Bartimaeus publicly identified him as the son of David in a manner that Jesus could neither ignore nor refuse. Jesus had to be aware of the persistent whispers among the crowd on the ascent with him. As he nears Jerusalem Jesus may look for God's confirmation for a very public though subtle entry to the city as God's Messiah. He sends ahead for a colt. The colt is available as he has said. The plan is confirmed. So he enters Jerusalem riding the messianic colt. He accepts the crowd's acclaim as the anointed son of David. Thus, he enters Jerusalem acknowledged by some portion of the crowd as Messiah, although he does not yet make that claim about himself.

The next day in the temple Jesus asserts a messianic authority. In a public act he challenges a practice that has the blessings of the high priest by driving out those who are doing prescribed business in the temple, and he makes the claim that God's temple is intended for another use. It is to be a house of prayer for all people. Then at the fig tree he instructs his own about prayer, inviting them to a more trusting relationship with God and to live continuously and consciously in the presence of the Father.

Jesus will go on to tell a story, the parable of the vineyard, in which he offers an interpretation of the Messiah. A few days hence Jesus will not recoil but claim directly to the high priest that he is the Messiah, the Son of God. In the meantime, by his teaching and by handling challenging questions with precision and force, Jesus demonstrates his continuing authority in the temple.

Mark Chapter 12

Jesus has just outplayed the temple leadership over a simple question on their own turf, the temple courtyard. Treading lightly, they did not send the temple police immediately to arrest him. In fact they came rather meekly, although in an assemblage of temple power, and actually asked Jesus on whose authority he does these things, disturbing the trade and the peace of the temple. By asking them a question of his own, Jesus entirely avoids giving them a direct answer, and thus also avoids debate over the content of the answer he would have given. Jesus now turns to tell a story.

> 12 Then he began to speak to them in parables. "A man planted a vineyard, put a fence around it, dug a pit for the wine press, and built a watchtower; then he leased it to tenants and went to another country. 2 When the season came, he sent a slave to the tenants to collect from them his share of the produce of the vineyard. 3 But they seized him, and beat him, and sent him away empty-handed. 4 And again he sent another slave to them; this one they beat over the head and insulted. 5 Then he sent another, and that one they killed. And so it was with many others; some they beat, and others they killed. 6 He had still one other, a beloved son. Finally he sent him to them, saying, 'They will respect my son.' 7 But those tenants said to one another, 'This is the heir; come, let us kill him, and the inheritance will be ours.' 8 So they seized him, killed him, and threw him out of the vineyard. 9 What then will the owner of the vineyard do? He will come and destroy the tenants and give the vineyard to others. 10 Have you not read this scripture:
>
> > 'The stone that the builders rejected
> > has become the cornerstone;

**11 this was the Lord's doing,
and it is amazing in our eyes.'?"**

It is the story of intrigue, of human greed that affects the thinking of some tenants, mixed with shrewd thinking over how to turn the Law to one's own advantage. If the temple leadership want to leave, they are also drawn back to the circle to listen, to hear how this one will turn out.

Jesus tells the practical details of a man who planted a vineyard: he puts a low stone wall around it, builds a wine press and a tower, and then he leases the vineyard to tenants while he goes to another country. He has become an absentee landlord. Galilean peasants commonly resented the many absentee landowners in their district. The owner of this vineyard, when the time comes, sends for his share of the harvest.

The tenants take advantage of the fact that the owner is far away. There is a law that states that under specific circumstances an inheritance may be regarded as ownerless property. If there is no heir it may be claimed by anyone, and the prior right belongs to the claimant who comes first. As current workers, the tenants want to claim the vineyard as their own.[1] So they delay sending the owner's share of the produce to him. They abuse his servants and kill his son. Perhaps they think the owner is too old or too busy to come to the vineyard himself.

**12 When they realized that he had told this parable against
them, they wanted to arrest him, but they feared the crowd.
So they left him and went away.**

How does Jesus suddenly turn the story on the leaders of the temple? Even granting that Jerusalem leaders make up an important portion of the Jewish absentee landowner class and the fact that many of the listeners are peasants is not enough to turn tables here, because the story takes the vantage of the owner from the beginning. What happens in Jesus' telling is that the one who was first simply identified as "a man (*anthropos*)" who planted the vineyard is suddenly called "the lord (*kurios*) of the vineyard."[2] This is juxtaposed in the next breath with a quote from Psalm 118:22–23 in which the Lord God (*kuriou*) will turn a rejected stone into the cornerstone of the entire structure.

---

1. Jeremias, *Parables of Jesus*, 75; *Jerusalem in the Time of Jesus*, 327–28.
2. NRSV translates this phrase as "owner of the vineyard" instead of "lord of the vineyard" which makes us miss the linguistic point. The Nestle-Aland Greek text has "*kurios*" in verse 9.

"Follow Me."

Almost simultaneously the crowd and the religious leaders realize that the story is a parable about God's judgment upon those who refuse to recognize God's envoys. The leaders who have not even dared to say that John the Baptist was God's servant must resist the claim that Jesus comes with God's authority. How could they answer such a parable? To deal with it is already to admit that it applies to themselves. They have to walk away.

The parable's judgment upon the tenants is severe: they will be destroyed and the vineyard given to others. As the leaders take their leave we can reflect further on this parable. In context, the parable makes Jesus himself the beloved Son who comes with his Father's authority. Because Jesus hints that he is the cornerstone we can see the story as an interpretation of his acclaimed entry to Jerusalem on the colt. He is God's envoy, the Messiah. In fact Jesus will suffer every violence the tenants hand out in the story, and more besides. He will be seized, beaten, wounded in the head, insulted, and killed.

This parable marks a turning point. The religious leaders refuse to recognize Jesus' claim to authority in Jerusalem. They are driven to challenge Jesus and to take matters into their own hands.

> **13 Then they sent to him some Pharisees and some Herodians to trap him in what he said. 14 And they came and said to him, "Teacher, we know that you are sincere, and show deference to no one; for you do not regard people with partiality, but teach the way of God in accordance with truth. Is it lawful to pay taxes to the emperor, or not? 15 Should we pay them, or should we not?" But knowing their hypocrisy, he said to them, "Why are you putting me to the test? Bring me a denarius and let me see it." 16 And they brought one. Then he said to them, "Whose head is this, and whose title?" They answered, "The emperor's." 17 Jesus said to them, "Give to the emperor the things that are the emperor's, and to God the things that are God's." And they were utterly amazed at him.**

Note that the questioners are Pharisees and Herodians, the same coalition of church and state that conspired against Jesus (in 3:6) after Jesus healed the man with the withered hand. They butter Jesus up before asking him the question. "Should we pay taxes to Caesar?"[3]

---

3. Julius Caesar's family name was adapted by his successors and came to be a title equivalent to the title of emperor. Knox, "Caesar," 478.

Mark Chapter 12

It is a hostile question, but one that was much discussed by people of that time and by tax resisters even today. It is one of those questions that will get you coming or going. The zealots of Galilee claimed that a Jew cannot pay taxes to Caesar and remain a Jew. Herod collected more taxes on top of Caesar's for his own building programs. The people hate the "treasonous" Jewish tax collectors. They sympathize with the zealots but most of them, like most of us, pay their taxes. If Jesus answers, "Yes, pay taxes to Caesar," he can be accused of teaching submission to Caesar rather than God and he undermines some of his popular support by the people. If Jesus says, "Do not pay Caesar," he can be accused of subverting the Roman Empire. To be sure, the Herodians and Pharisees are listening very carefully for his answer.

Tax payment was made in Roman coin. Jesus calls for a denarius. The questioners produce the coin, a coin that some Pharisees will not even want to touch. Jesus holds out the coin.

"Whose head is this?" Jesus asks.

The image engraved on the coin, Caesar's head, was counted a matter of idolatry by the most devout Jews. It was a graven image prohibited by the second commandment (Exod 20:4, RSV). The inscription on the denarius reads: "August and Divine Son." The questioners reply, "Caesar's." In the RSV translation Jesus answers,

"Render to Caesar the things that are Caesar's, and to God the things that are God's" (Mark 12:17, RSV).

A powerful answer!—particularly when we consider what Jesus teaches us by example to give God. The Pharisees and Herodians are stunned. So the Sadducees come up with their question to stump the rabbi.

> 18 Some of the Sadducees, who say there is no resurrection, came to him and asked him a question, saying, 19 "Teacher, Moses wrote for us that 'if a man's brother dies, leaving a wife but no child, the man shall marry the widow and raise up children for his brother.' 20 There were seven brothers; the first married and, when he died, left no children; 21 and the second married her and died, leaving no children; and the third likewise; 22 none of the seven left children. Last of all the woman herself died. 23 In the resurrection whose wife will she be? For the seven had married her."

This was a hypothetical question for the Sadducees, the sort of question they have used to confound those who teach belief in the resurrection. The command to provide for the widow in this manner is found in the Torah, in Deuteronomy 25:5–6. The Sadducees held that the Torah, the five books of Moses, provides the Scripture of highest authority. They interpreted it quite literally, and found nothing about resurrection in the Torah. On the other hand, Jewish proponents of resurrection found their sources in late apocryphal and apocalyptic writings such as Daniel 12:2 instead of the early portions of Jewish Scripture.

Jesus takes on the Sadducees with a direct challenge. "You are wrong!"

> **24 Jesus said to them, "Is not this the reason you are wrong, that you know neither the scriptures nor the power of God? 25 For when they rise from the dead, they neither marry nor are given in marriage, but are like angels in heaven. 26 And as for the dead being raised, have you not read in the book of Moses, in the story about the bush, how God said to him, 'I am the God of Abraham, the God of Isaac, and the God of Jacob'? 27 He is God not of the dead, but of the living; you are quite wrong."**

Jesus speaks of God's power to raise persons from the dead. He asserts with authority that, once raised, humans do not marry as we do on earth but are like angels in the presence of God. Then, providing a basis in Scripture for belief in the resurrection, Jesus reaches into the heart of the Torah to the story where God speaks to Moses out of the burning bush (Exod 3:6). All parties to this debate grant that God exists. Jesus quotes God's claim, "I *am* the God of Abraham, of Isaac, and of Jacob." Jesus concludes that not only does God live but Abraham, Isaac, and Jacob are alive as well!

> **28 One of the scribes came near and heard them disputing with one another, and seeing that he answered them well, he asked him, "Which commandment is the first of all?" 29 Jesus answered, "The first is, 'Hear, O Israel: The Lord our God, the Lord is one; 30 you shall love the Lord your God with all your heart, and with all your soul, and with all your mind, and with all your strength.' 31 The second is this, 'You shall love your neighbor as yourself.' There is no other commandment greater than these."**

A sympathetic scribe, hearing how effectively Jesus answers his challengers, asks Jesus the traditional puzzle, to identify the first and greatest commandment. The rich man had come to Jesus with a similar question. Jesus gives the scribe two quotes from the Torah. First is the Shema: "Hear O Israel: The Lord our God, the Lord is one; you shall love the Lord your God with all your heart, and soul, and strength" which comes from Deuteronomy 6:4-5, to which Jesus adds "and with all your mind." This states in practical positive terms what would be involved in taking to heart the first four commandments of the Decalogue, those that focus specifically on humans in covenant relationship with God. The second comes from Leviticus 19:18. And if you actually do love your neighbor in a manner that complements your love for yourself, you will fulfill the final six commandments of the Decalogue which involve a covenant relationship with community members. This would put the prophetic call to a humble honesty, justice, and mercy into practice. The two portions of Jesus' summary together embody what the prophet Jeremiah calls for when he teaches that God will write the covenant on the hearts of his people.[4]

> **32 Then the scribe said to him, "You are right, Teacher; you have truly said that 'he is one, and besides him there is no other'; 33 and 'to love him with all the heart, and with all the understanding, and with all the strength' and 'to love one's neighbor as oneself,'—this is much more important than all whole burnt offerings and sacrifices." 34 When Jesus saw that he answered wisely, he said to him, "You are not far from the kingdom of God." After that no one dared to ask him any question.**

To know this is to be close to the kingdom of God. To practice it in daily life is to live in the kingdom. "You are close." As in his answer to the rich man, Jesus speaks with the authority of one who knows and lives in the kingdom of God.

> **35 While Jesus was teaching in the temple, he said, "How can the scribes say that the Messiah is the son of David? 36 David himself, by the Holy Spirit, declared,**
>   **'The Lord said to my Lord,**
>   **"Sit at my right hand,**
>   **until I put your enemies under your feet."' 37 David himself calls him 'Lord;' so how can he be his son?" And the large crowd was listening to him with delight.**

---

4. Jeremiah 31:33. Once again Jesus has referred to that portion of Leviticus, 19:11-18, which, along with the Decalogue, his brother James calls "the royal law" or "the law of the kingdom," in James 2:8. Johnson, *Brother of Jesus*, 123-35.

"Follow Me."

Jesus pulls out a puzzle for the Jerusalem scribes, the supreme experts in interpreting biblical passages. The puzzle is about the Messiah, a puzzle in interpreting Psalm 110:1.

The scribes do not want to answer any questions about the Messiah at the moment. This question ties back in to the messianic procession into Jerusalem. Is the kingdom coming as David's kingdom or as an alternative kingdom? As to the puzzle itself: the Messiah is to be a son of David. Why does David call him Lord (*kurios*) in this Psalm? Because the Messiah is greater than David. The Messiah's authority, the Messiah's kingdom is therefore greater than David's kingdom. By implication, the listeners are asked to accept the authority and the vision Jesus provides, if he is the Messiah as his acts in Jerusalem maintain. Jesus presents a choice. Once again Jesus speaks with an authority that delights the crowd.

> **38 As he taught, he said, "Beware of the scribes, who like to walk around in long robes, and to be greeted with respect in the marketplaces, 39 and to have the best seats in the synagogues and places of honor at banquets! 40 They devour widows' houses and for the sake of appearance say long prayers. They will receive the greater condemnation."**

Now we get a direct attack on some of the sins of the scribes. There is no one easier to make fun of than a self-righteous person of piety. But Jesus is dead serious in his attack. They act in exactly the manner that Jesus has been trying—with only moderate, if any, success—to teach his disciples not to act, living the values of this world while dressed in religious garb. The list is delightfully long: long robes, greeted with respect, best seats, and places of honor.

Verse 40 may allude to the practice of scribal trusteeship. A widow could not legally manage her husband's estates. Scribes or priests could be made trustees of those estates and would get a legitimate percentage of the income for their labor. The practice was open to embezzlement and abuse.

Note that each of the important groups of temple leadership has been unable to confront Jesus effectively. Their questions have been turned against them and they have not been able to respond: the contingent of chief priests and elders, the Pharisees and Herodians, the Sadducees, and the scribes. Time and again, Jesus has attacked them directly and indirectly as he teaches. Who is left to defend the temple?

> 41 He sat down opposite the treasury, and watched the crowd putting money into the treasury. Many rich people put in large sums. 42 A poor widow came and put in two small copper coins, which are worth a penny. 43 Then he called his disciples and said to them, "Truly I tell you, this poor widow has put in more than all those who are contributing to the treasury. 44 For all of them have contributed out of their abundance; but she out of her poverty has put in everything she had, all she had to live on."

In a quiet scene with his disciples after the flurry of temple exchanges Jesus sits opposite the temple treasury. Jesus sees a widow put in two *lepta*, the smallest coin in circulation. To the surprise of his disciples, Jesus once again draws attention to one of the little, a weak one, the person in need. Jesus finds victory here. This widow is the one person who gave everything she had. She *is* one who, giving all to God, will find life (8:35), who enacts her love for God in giving her full measure (4:24; 12:30). It is a fitting cap to Jesus' instruction to his servant community.

Mark Chapter 13

13 As he came out of the temple, one of his disciples said to him, "Look, Teacher, what large stones and what large buildings!" 2 Then Jesus asked him, "Do you see these great buildings? Not one stone will be left here upon another; all will be thrown down."

THE PARABLE OF THE wicked tenants contained its warning (12:9). And if God's judgment did not stand out in the allusion to Jeremiah when he cleared the temple courtyard (11:17), Jesus here declares that the temple itself will be utterly destroyed. "Do you see (in Greek, *blepeis*) these great stones?" When he taught with parables Jesus repeatedly used verbs from the auditory sense to focus our attention, "If you have ears to hear, listen!" In this chapter Jesus will repeatedly use the Greek verb *blepo*, to look, to direct the eyes on something to see it, using the visual sense for a similar effect. In the context that follows it becomes a kind of warning for disciples. Look actively, look carefully, *blepete*; and is appropriately translated, "beware."

3 When he was sitting on the Mount of Olives, opposite the Temple, Peter, James, John, and Andrew asked him privately, 4 "Tell us, when will this be, and what will be the sign that all these things are about to be accomplished?" 5 Then Jesus began to say to them, "Beware, that no one leads you astray. 6 Many will come in my name and say, "I am he!" and they will lead many astray.

The confrontations in Jerusalem, even the claim that the beautiful buildings will be destroyed, occurred in a public forum where anybody could listen and jump in with a challenge. The remainder of chapter 13 presents a closed discourse between Jesus and his disciples. As if to emphasize the intimacy of this dialogue, the questions are asked by an inner circle, the first four disciples who followed him. We get the impression that Jesus and the twelve have left the city, traversed the Kidron Valley, and pause to rest as they climb the Mount of Olives. They turn to look back to see Jerusalem on the opposite summit. From this vantage the temple is visible over the city walls. It is a quiet moment that invites reflection. Just as they did in coming down the mountain after the transfiguration (9:11), the disciples probe for details. When will this judgment pronounced on the temple take place? How will we know that the time is near?

Jesus does not give a direct answer for either the time or sign they ask for. He seems to have an entirely different agenda in mind. "*Blepete* (Watch out!) lest you be led astray." Watch out for false prophets. Jesus has not gone about the country claiming to be the Messiah. His approach has been to allow the power of God to be demonstrated through him, acting with confidence at the moment a person in need crosses his path. His teaching has focused on God's forgiving and God's judgment and what it means for us to serve God and others. When Jesus has spoken of his own task he generally speaks in the third person of the Son of Man (e.g. 2:10; 8:31). After he asked his disciples, "Who do you say that I am?" (8:29), he sternly ordered them not to tell anyone. On his entrance to Jerusalem Jesus did not request, but he did not hinder, the cries of the people waving branches and shouting "Blessed is he who comes in the name of the Lord." Even while acting with messianic authority in the temple over the past few days, Jesus has avoided the outright claim, "I am the Messiah!" But he now warns his disciples that others will claim to be the messiah, saying, "I am he," or in Greek, *ego eimi*.

The phrase *ego eimi* occurs three times in Mark, each time on Jesus' lips. In Mark 6:50 when the disciples were fighting a strong wind on the Sea of Galilee, Jesus frightened them while walking on the water. "Do not be afraid," he called to them. "Take heart. It is I [*ego eimi*]." This would be the common, everyday use of the verb "to be," first person singular, *ego*, I, *eimi*, am. Are you he? or Are you she? can be answered, *ego eimi*, "I am." Who is there? "It is I," *ego eimi*. On the other hand, here (13:6) we find that the phrase can be used to make an additional claim about oneself, saying "I am he," *ego eimi*, and meaning "I am the Messiah," or perhaps the much stronger "I am God." Where do the Jews find *that* kind of content to fill the words, "I am"?

"Follow Me."

We must digress to examine this phrase in detail because it will be involved when the high priest accuses Jesus of blasphemy. The phrase *ego eimi* is used both by humans and by God in the Greek translation of Jewish Scripture, the Septuagint. Joseph tells his brothers, "I am [*ego eimi*] Joseph" (Gen 45:3–4). Abraham said to the Hittites when he wanted to buy a cave in which to bury Sarah, "I am [*ego eimi*] a stranger and an alien residing among you" (Gen 23:4). God tells Abraham, "I am [*ego eimi*] your God" (Gen 17:1), and says to Isaac, "I am [*ego eimi*] the God of your father Abraham. Do not be afraid" (Gen 26:24). These exemplify the everyday use of the verb.

On the other hand, when God speaks from the burning bush to Moses God says in Hebrew, *"Ehyeh asher ehyeh,"* which is a cryptic saying using the same form of the verb *to be* twice. This is translated into English as "I am who I am" or "I am what I am" or "I will be what I will be" (Exod 3:14). The Septuagint translates the Hebrew phrase into Greek by using two forms of the verb *to be, ego eimi ho on*, which comes out in English as "I am the one who is." In this context the phrase *ego eimi* is at least closely associated with the name of God and is to be understood as revealing God's name and nature.

Occasionally God uses the self-descriptive phrase *ego eimi* as an absolute name for God. In Deuteronomy 32:39 God says, "See now that *ego eimi*," which can be translated "See that I am He," or alternatively, "See that I am God." In Isaiah 43:25, the phrase is doubled, *ego eimi ego eimi*, meaning, "I am God," or "I am I Am who blots out your transgressions." Isaiah twice quotes God saying, "I am God [*ego eimi ho theos*], and there is no other" (Isa 45:22; 46:9). However, perhaps in sacrilegious play, certainly in arrogance, the young woman who personifies Babylon twice claims, "I am [*ego eimi*] and there is no one besides me" (Isa 47:8, 10). If this is understood as Babylon strutting as if in conquest of Israel's God, for she has conquered Israel, the claim would be blasphemous.

Turning again to the scene on the Mount of Olives, Jesus warns his disciples that pretenders will use the phrase *ego eimi* in making a false claim to be the Messiah. The words themselves do not guarantee the claim. Keep your eyes open for such teachers. Jesus' third use of *ego eimi* will occur in 14:62, which we shall come to in short order.

Jesus then seems to steer back toward the question about the destruction of the temple but now draws a focus that pushes the time line into a distant future.

> 7 "When you hear of wars and rumors of wars, do not be alarmed; this must take place, but the end is still to come. 8 For nation will rise against nation, and kingdom against kingdom; there will be earthquakes in various places; there will be famines. This is but the beginning of the birthpangs."

Jesus enumerates numerous catastrophes that will affect many people, not only the disciples. This seems, in effect, an admonition to his followers not to get soft, not to go lazy while waiting for God's judgment to fall on others. He wants them to be actively engaged, to be strong, to be true, now and for the long haul. There will be wars and rumors of wars, various conflicts between kingdoms, as well as earthquakes, and famines. Do not be overly alarmed at these. Such catastrophes must (*dei*) take place. Some considerable time will pass. But *oupo to telos*, "not yet the end."

The image of a mother enduring birth pangs suggests that there is a direction to the wait, a purpose for our suffering. Birthpangs come before the gift of a child held in its mother's arms. God's plan involves a gift yet to come.

> 9 "As for yourselves, beware; for they will hand you over to councils; and you will be beaten in synagogues; and you will stand before governors and kings because of me, as a testimony to them. 10 And the good news must first be proclaimed to all nations. 11 When they bring you to trial and hand you over, do not worry beforehand about what you are to say; but say whatever is given to you at that time, for it is not you who speak, but the Holy Spirit. 12 Brother will betray brother to death, and a father his child, and children will rise against parents and have them put to death; 13 and you will be hated by all because of my name. But the one who endures to the end will be saved."

Jesus now turns with instructions specifically for his disciples. To paraphrase, "You who would follow me, beware." *Blepete*. "You must be ready to suffer for me." Jesus prepares disciples for their task in the present age.

"Follow Me."

The kingdom of God may be present in your lives but the promised age to come has not fully arrived. The good news must (*dei*) still be shared with the rest of the world. Remember whose you are. You will stand witness for me. You will face authorities at local, regional, and national levels and suffer physically because of my name. There will be hatred for you and betrayal even among family members because of me.

Why should Jesus expect his disciples to have to face such burdens? Every act of redemption incurs some cost. Remember that in sharing the good news Jesus invites us to join God's kingdom, which begins with a call to repentance (Mark 1:14–15). We realize that none of us has lived up to God's standards. What some people will accept as good news while honestly repenting, others will reject as a threat to their chosen way of life. In addition, there is a certain cost incurred whenever a person gives of herself or himself, even in the pursuit of a life doing good things for others. This is the cost of serving others. Jesus does not say that every one who follows him will suffer in the extreme but warns disciples to be ready to accept the suffering that may be required. This is the cost of redemption in the broad sense that we can understand Jesus' everyday actions to be redemptive (10:45).

Jesus insists that the good news he brings must (*dei*) be proclaimed to all nations. Every human that can be reached should be given the invitation. This is the task his followers are to be involved in. Jesus leads the way by example in preaching the good news and God's judgment, by serving others at almost every step, and by his willingness to take on himself the suffering entailed by the confrontation of love with evil. That is God's plan. But do not worry overmuch ahead of time when you must stand in witness. God's Holy Spirit will speak through you. It is promised.

> **14 "But when you see the desolating sacrilege set up where it ought not to be (let the reader understand), then those in Judea must flee to the mountains; 15 the one on the housetop must not go down or enter the house to take anything away; 16 the one in the field must not turn back to get a coat. 17 Woe to those who are pregnant and to those who are nursing infants in those days! 18 Pray that it may not be in winter. 19 For in those days there will be suffering, such as has not been from the beginning of the creation that God created until now, no, and never will be. 20 And**

if the Lord had not cut short those days, no one would be saved; but for the sake of the elect, whom he chose, he has cut short those days. 21 And if anyone says to you at that time, "Look! Here is the Messiah!" or "Look! There he is!"—do not believe it. 22 False messiahs and false prophets will appear and produce signs and omens, to lead astray, if possible, the elect. 23 But be alert; I have already told you everything."

"Desolating sacrilege" was the phrase used to describe the desecration of the temple when Antiochus Epiphanes conquered Jerusalem, and completed the act by sacrificing swine to Zeus on the sacred altar of the temple in 167 BCE (Dan 11:31; 1 Macc 1:54–56). Antiochus Epiphanes enforced his decree that anyone found possessing a copy of the covenant or caught practicing the Law of Moses would be put to death. There were Jewish martyrs. Three years later Judas Maccabeus led an armed revolt that freed the temple and led to quasi-independence from Syria. Jewish kings and high priests of the Hasmonian family held power for 100 years until the Roman conquest in 63 BCE. The Maccabean revolt provided a concrete model for Jewish messianic movements during the next 200 years.

"Flee to the mountains when the desolating sacrilege is set up where it must (*dei*) not be." What is the reader, whom Mark addresses parenthetically, to understand? Jesus expects another conquest of Jerusalem, complete with its temple desecration. He urges his own not to resist by force but to flee the suffering that will come.[1] And again Jesus warns against being led astray by false messiahs. Keep your eyes open! Be alert! *Blepete!*

24 "But in those days, after that suffering,
the sun will be darkened,
and the moon will not give its light,
25 and the stars will be falling from heaven,
and the powers in the heavens will be shaken.
26 Then they will see 'the Son of Man coming in clouds' with great power and glory. 27 Then he will send out the angels, and gather his elect from the four winds, from the ends of the earth to the ends of heaven."

---

1. Mark's (and Matthew's) imagery is based on the earlier (167 BCE) conquest of Jerusalem. The same admonition in Luke more concretely describes armies surrounding Jerusalem.

"FOLLOW ME."

With these words Jesus projects his vision beyond destruction of the temple. The apocalyptic literature of his day commonly included celestial portents, such as the shaking of the heavens, as signs of God's ultimate control. In the midst of such a scene Jesus describes his vision of a truly victorious Messiah, one that reaches beyond Peter's wish for an immediate human victory, even, perhaps, beyond the confines of our earth. Victory is promised for God's Messiah using not Daniel's indefinite "a son of man" but Jesus' label for himself: "the Son of Man will come in the clouds with power and glory to gather his elect." This is a promise of his return, the kingdom of God in triumphant power and in glory!

The Daniel passage alluded to, with God described as the Ancient of Days, reads:

> 13 I saw in the night, visions, and behold,
> with the clouds of heaven there came one like a son of man,
> and he came to the Ancient of Days and was presented before him.
> 14 And to him was given dominion and glory and kingdom,
> that all peoples, nations and languages should serve him;
> his dominion is an everlasting dominion, which shall not pass away,
> and his kingdom one that shall not be destroyed.
>
> (Dan 7:13–14, RSV)

Jesus turns next to the image of a fig tree.

> **28 "From the fig tree learn its lesson: as soon as its branch becomes tender and puts forth its leaves, you know that summer is near. 29 So also, when you see these things taking place, you know that he is near, at the very gates. 30 Truly I tell you, this generation will not pass away until all these things have taken place. 31 Heaven and earth will pass away, but my words will not pass away."**

Jesus uses the fig tree as a metaphor. But what is near is not so clear from Mark's Greek text. The verb *to be*, third person singular, is used in two consecutive sentences: first, "summer [it] is near;" and in the next we have not "he is near" but simply the verb without an explicit reference, "[he, she, or it] is near." The phrase "pressing on the door" may imply that a personal being, God or the Messiah, is at the gate.

Because verse 32 will address the matter of time, the metaphor of the fig tree implies that the events he has described can be taken as signs, and that Jesus is dealing with the questions the four disciples raised in verse 4. Jesus has described events that will happen in the time to come after his death and resurrection, statements grouped by their application to humans generally, to the disciples in particular, to the destruction of Jerusalem, and to the victorious return of the true Messiah. These events are meant to be at least loose antecedents to a triumphant kingdom in God's presence.

The claim, "this generation will not pass until all these things have taken place," is proven to be false if it meant that the earth itself was to end eighty years after Jesus died. The image of sun and moon made dark had been used by several prophets in warning the Jews and the nations of God's impending judgment, the Day of the Lord (see Isa 13:9–11; Ezek 32:7–8; Joel 2:1–2, 10, 30–31). On the other hand, focusing on the disciples immediately in front of Jesus, before that generation would pass on there would be wars and Jerusalem and the temple would be destroyed; the disciples met with the resurrected Jesus, became witnesses for him, and some suffered martyrdom. There may also be a sense in which God's judgment is continually imminent.

To the factual question the disciples asked, however, Jesus now answers that when this is to take place, temporally speaking, is known only to God the Father. This is an important qualification to any claim about the kingdom of God in its fullness. Jesus' words can be trusted, his promises will endure. His followers are to trust until the Father's victory comes. But keep alert! *Blepete!*

> **32 "But about that day or hour no one knows, neither the angels in heaven, nor the Son, but only the Father. 33 Beware, keep alert; for you do not know when the time will come. 34 It is like a man going on a journey, when he leaves home and puts his slaves in charge, each with his work, and commands the doorkeeper to be on the watch. 35 Therefore, keep awake—for you do not know when the master of the house will come, in the evening, or at midnight, or at cockcrow, or at dawn, 36 or else he may find you asleep when he comes suddenly. 37 And what I say to you I say to all: keep awake."**

Jesus ends this teaching with a parable about a landowner going away and returning. Since Jesus has just promised that he will return in glory it seems to be another parable on himself. Each servant is given a task. The master wants the servants to keep him in mind during his absence. It is interesting that in this parable a new sensory verb is used, three times, to command alertness: *gregoreo*, (to wake up, to keep awake, to keep watch, to be vigilant and attentive). There is a subtle change in perspective here. The servant is not just to observe events unfolding in the world with a discriminating eye. The servant is to maintain an active vigilance concerning his or her own task in the master's household. Keep watch! Stay awake! *Greigoreite!*

It is worth noticing that this entire Mount of Olives dialogue, which involves threats and promises that are yet to come, points the disciples and the reader to a time that extends beyond Jesus' death and resurrection, far beyond the ending of the book of Mark. Mark expects that Jesus' story will be of value beyond the words of his text.

Mark Chapter 14

14 It was two days before the Passover and the festival of Unleavened Bread. The chief priests and the scribes were looking for a way to arrest Jesus by stealth and kill him; 2 for they said, "Not during the festival, or there may be a riot among the people."

THE PASSOVER AND THE seven-day Festival of Unleavened Bread memorialize God's act of freeing the children of Israel from slavery to the Egyptians in the tenth plague God used when Pharoah refused to let the Israelites go. Exodus 12:1—13:10 spells out instructions for how the Passover was to take place. The Israelites, many of whom were still shepherds, were to slay a year-old lamb without blemish on the designated day, take some of its blood and mark the two doorposts and the lintel of their homes with the blood. The lamb's bones were not to be broken. Families or groups of people were to roast the lamb and eat it that night. And that night, "when he sees the blood on the lintel and the two doorposts, the Lord will pass over that door and will not allow the destroyer to enter your houses to strike you down" (Exod 12:23). The firstborn sons of the Egyptians, however, were struck down. Passover came to be the first day of the seven days of the Festival of Unleavened Bread. No leaven was to be used during the festival, to commemorate the quick exodus of the Israelites from their homes in Egypt. These festivals were to be celebrated and passed down by Jews from generation to generation.

In Jesus' day the Passover lamb was to be slain in the temple and the Passover meal eaten inside Jerusalem. A single lamb would feed a group of ten or more persons. A multitude of pilgrims from the diaspora and nearby

"Follow Me."

lands would come to Jerusalem, making Passover the largest festival of the year. Lambs without blemish and other offerings were sold in the Court of the Gentiles around the temple. Men would be seen carrying a lamb on their shoulders, taking it to a priest. The priest would sprinkle some of the lamb's blood on the altar.

Why a lamb's blood? "It is the Passover sacrifice to the Lord, for he passed over the houses of the Israelites in Egypt, when he struck down the Egyptians but spared our houses" (Exod 12:27). Every act of redemption involves some cost or sacrifice. The Israelites accepted this sacrifice when they marked their doors with the lambs' blood. At the burning bush God had said to Moses "I am the Lord, and I will free you from the burdens of the Egyptians and deliver you from slavery to them. I will redeem you with an outstretched arm and with mighty acts of judgment" (Exod 6:6). In retrospect, after crossing the Red Sea, Moses and the people sing a song of joy, "In your steadfast love you led the people whom you redeemed" (Exod 15:13). These verses use the uniquely Hebrew notion of *goel* for God here, speaking of God as a kinsman who redeems his people. Centuries later, during another time of forced exile in Babylon, the prophet Isaiah will repeatedly call the exiles in Babylon to return to Jerusalem using the same intimate terms. "Thus says the Lord, your Redeemer" (Isa 44:24); "return to me, for I have redeemed you" (Isa 44:22).

> **3 While he was at Bethany in the house of Simon the leper, as he sat at the table, a woman came with an alabaster jar of very costly ointment of nard, and she broke open the jar and poured the ointment on his head. 4 But some were there who said to one another in anger, "Why was the ointment wasted in this way? 5 For this ointment could have been sold for more than three hundred denarii, and the money given to the poor." And they scolded her. 6 But Jesus said, "Let her alone. Why do you trouble her? She has performed a good service for me. 7 For you always have the poor with you, and you can show kindness to them whenever you wish; but you will not always have me. 8 She has done what she could; she has anointed my body beforehand for its burial. 9 Truly I tell you, wherever the good news is proclaimed in the whole world, what she has done will be told in remembrance of her."**

We do not know Simon, but his designation as a leper reminds us of Jesus healing lepers and the social barriers that Jesus often breaks down. Nor is the woman who boldly pours a costly oil over Jesus' head identified by name in Mark (but see John 12:1-8). The nard is worth roughly a laborer's wages for a year. Some unidentified observers are indignant. Jesus listens to their rebuke. As in his earlier responses to the paralytic and to the children (Mark 2:1-12; 10:13-16) Jesus directs his attention to the woman who is suddenly the focus of everyone's attention, then to the opponents, and back with an affirmation of the woman. Once again he lifts one of the least to a position of honor. "She who anoints me" affirms her act. "Messiah" means "anointed one" in Hebrew. To the surprise of everyone including the woman, Jesus takes this opportunity to declare his commitment to pursue his mission through an upcoming death and burial before a larger audience than his immediate disciples. What this woman has done, Jesus insists, will be remembered wherever his story is told!

> **10 Then Judas Iscariot, who was one of the twelve, went to the chief priests in order to betray him to them. 11 When they heard it, they were greatly pleased, and promised to give him money. So he began to look for an opportunity to betray him.**

This chapter opens with the chief priests and their associates seeking the opportunity to take Jesus and kill him. When Judas Iscariot appears, his proposal readily fits their desires. Now Judas quietly looks for his moment to betray his teacher.

In stark contrast to the woman who pours out her costly gift of oil, Judas will sell out to the chief priests for money. Mark expresses distress at the tragedy that Jesus is betrayed by a member of his inner community in a subtle way. Mark uses the phrase "one of the twelve" three times in this chapter, once on Jesus' lips (14:10, 20, 43), and he uses some form of the verb "to betray" seven times in this chapter, four times on Jesus' lips (14:10, 11, 18, 21, 41, 42, 44).

> **12 On the first day of Unleavened Bread, when the Passover lamb is sacrificed, his disciples said to him, "Where do you want us to go and make the preparations for you to eat the Passover?" 13 So he sent two of his disciples, saying to them, "Go into the city, and a man carrying a jar of water will meet you; follow him, 14 and wherever he enters, say**

"Follow Me."

> to the owner of the house, 'The Teacher asks, Where is my guest room where I may eat the Passover with my disciples?' 15 He will show you a large room upstairs, furnished and ready. Make preparations for us there." 16 So the disciples set out and went into the city, and found everything as he had told them; and they prepared the Passover meal.

A Middle-Eastern man would seldom carry a jug of water in the streets. That was considered woman's work. However, in an important exception to this practice, a pious Essene man would carry water for ritual cleansing. No woman was allowed to touch the ritual water. One source of ritual water was the Pool of Siloam, which lies near the southeast gate of Jerusalem, an area where Essenes are believed to have lived. The disciples may have followed an Essene and prepared the Passover meal in the guest room of an Essene.[1]

> 17 When it was evening, he came with the twelve. 18 And when they had taken their places and were eating, Jesus said, "Truly I tell you, one of you will betray me, one who is eating with me." 19 They began to be distressed and to say to him one after another, "Surely, not I?" 20 He said to them, "It is one of the twelve, one who is dipping bread into the bowl with me. 21 For the Son of Man goes as it is written of him, but woe to that one by whom the Son of Man is betrayed! It would have been better for that one not to have been born."

The disciples have taken their places and are reclining around a low table to eat the Passover meal with Jesus. A common meal, and particularly the Passover meal, is among the most intimate forms of fellowship that friends can share. Jesus has been controversial in part because he has deliberately shared meals with a variety of outcasts and sinners.

The bowl into which members of this fellowship now dip contains a fruit puree that is to be eaten with bitter herbs, vegetables, and slices of fruit during the preliminary course of a Passover meal. The bitter herbs symbolize the bitter misery of slave labor; puree, the mortar used to bind Egyptian bricks; vegetables and fruit, the new season and hope for a better future.

---

1. Riesner, "Jesus," 219. The Essenes were one of the groups of priests mentioned in the discussion of Mark 2:17.

Jesus shares a bitter thing he knows with them, that one of his disciples is set to betray him, one who dips into the bowl with him.

Jesus eats with his betrayer. Handing one's host over to an enemy will be a deep violation of this fellowship. The disciples grieve to hear what Jesus says. They become distressed. The same verb was used to describe the rich man's consternation as he turned away from Jesus (10:22). In turn each disciple shows his human vulnerability, saying, *meiti ego?* "Who, me? How could I betray you? Certainly not I!"

Jesus asserts again that one of the twelve will betray him and contrasts this with his own faithfulness to his task, "For the Son of Man goes as it is written of him." He proceeds with a serious warning to the disciple who will betray him. "Woe to the one by whom the Son of Man is betrayed! It would have been better for that man not to have been born."

As I see it, even at this point in time, the final meal, and even though Jesus finds the matter written in Scripture as God's plan, neither act is inevitable, neither act is fated nor causally predetermined. The Son of Man freely chooses to go forward with God's plan. And Judas is free to choose, but will betray him. Jesus does not condemn the betrayer but warns him there are dire consequences for such an act. A similar warning was given against anyone who causes a little child who believes to stumble (9:42).

> **22 While they were eating, he took a loaf of bread, and after blessing it he broke it, gave it to them, and said, "Take; this is my body." 23 Then he took a cup, and after giving thanks he gave it to them, and all of them drank from it. 24 He said to them, "This is my blood of the covenant, which is poured out for many. 25 Truly I tell you, I will never again drink of the fruit of the vine until that day when I drink it new in the kingdom of God."**

After a preliminary course that includes the retelling of the story of the exodus from Egypt, the main Passover meal begins with the blessing of the bread. This may be the point in time at which Jesus took the *matzah*, the unleavened bread, and praised God in blessing the loaf. Mark's verb here, *eulogeo*, reflects the "Blessed art Thou, O Lord " of the Hebrew prayer. Jesus broke the bread and gave it to them.

The *matzah* is a symbol of the haste of the Hebrew departure when they were freed from slavery in Egypt. The main course, Passover lamb, commemorates God's passing over the children of Israel to spare them from death. Together they celebrate God's deliverance.

"Follow Me."

At the end of the main meal and before the final psalm is sung, the Passover host gives thanks to God for the provisions of this meal as he blesses a cup of wine. Mark's use of the verb *eucharisteo* reflects this thanksgiving prayer. This may be the point at which Jesus took the cup and gave it to his disciples.

The three verbs used in the first act—took the bread, blessed, and broke it—are known from rabbinical literature as technical terms for the grace at table before the meal. Parallel verbs are used for the after-meal thanksgiving. Thus the very words that make up the Christian Eucharist depend on an earlier Jewish tradition.[2] Both gesture and word are coordinated in this tradition.

Jesus:	took bread	blessed it	broke it	gave it
	took the cup	gave thanks		gave it

Mark used the same verbs in his accounts of the feeding of the 5,000 and the 4,000.

In the two blessings Jesus adds a new dimension to the symbols of the Passover. The elements are made to represent Jesus' life, the substance of his obedience to his Father, and his gift to those who partake of the meal. The unleavened bread becomes his broken body. Jesus lifts the bread to the Father, blesses it, breaks the bread, and gives it to them, saying "This is my body." The disciples partake of the bread. Jesus lifts the cup filled with red wine to his Father, gives thanks, and gives it to them saying, "This is my blood of the covenant which is poured out for many." Jesus thus interprets the act of giving his life, a broken body, and the blood poured out in his death, as a covenant sacrifice on behalf of sinners. Its messianic significance is brought out in the promise that he will drink new wine in God's presence in God's kingdom. All twelve disciples drink from the cup.

In speaking of "my blood of the covenant poured out" Jesus alludes to an event that comes later in the exodus story (Exod 24:4–8). Israelites were gathered at the foot of Mount Sinai. Several oxen were killed as a sacrifice of well-being, their blood was collected, and Moses dashed a portion of the blood on an altar built nearby. Moses then took the book of the covenant and read it to the people. The people listened and responded saying, "All that the Lord has spoken we will do, and we will be obedient." Moses then dashed the remainder of the blood on the people, sealing the covenant between God and the people, and saying, "See the blood of the covenant that

---

2. Jeremias, *Eucharistic Words of Jesus*, 97, 109–10.

the Lord has made with you in accordance with all these words" (Exod 24:7–8).

Returning to the moment Jesus shares with his disciples, we might note that the Eucharist in Mark is given in the present tense. It is not simply a memorial. In this respect it is like Matthew 26:26–9. This contrasts with the memorial Eucharist of Luke 22:19–20 and Paul's description of it in 1 Corinthians 11:23–6 where Jesus instructs his disciples to celebrate the Eucharist "in remembrance of me." By analogy to the Passover meal, the Eucharist is to be passed on from generation to generation.

Mark's Eucharist looks not to the past but to the present and the future. In sharing the bread and cup, in sharing his body and his lifeblood, Jesus invites us, in the present tense, to participate with him in the task of proclaiming the good news, serving, healing, renewing, and suffering on behalf of the sins of the world. What we have witnessed as we followed close enough to observe Jesus' acts of love and challenge, the full range of his instructions and his abundantly shared life, these he presents to us as he breaks the bread and passes the cup.

> **26 When they had sung the hymn, they went out to the Mount of Olives. 27 And Jesus said to them, "You will all become deserters; for it is written,**
>
> **'I will strike the shepherd and the sheep will be scattered.'**
>
> **28 But after I am raised up, I will go before you to Galilee." 29 Peter said to him, "Even though all become deserters, I will not." 30 Jesus said to him, "Truly I tell you, this day, this very night, before the cock crows twice, you will deny me three times." 31 But he said vehemently, "Even though I must die with you, I will not deny you." And all of them said the same.**

The Hallel Psalms 113–118 have a prominent place in the Passover ritual. The last hymn sung at the table is probably Psalm 118 in which a human soul cries out in distress to God, but relying on God for renewed life and for God's victory.[3] The psalm begins and ends with the cry of a trusting servant: "O give thanks to the Lord for he is good; for his steadfast love endures forever."

---

3. Several verses of this psalm have played an important part in this Passover week (Ps 118:22–23; 25–26; Mark 12:10–11; 11:9–10).

"Follow Me."

After singing the psalm they leave Jerusalem, walk across the Kidron Valley and up the Mount of Olives. Jesus now tells the disciples, "You will be caused to stumble.[4] You will desert me, for it is written," and he quotes from Zechariah 13:7, "'I will strike the shepherd and the sheep will scatter.'" Jesus follows this with a promise that looks beyond the end of Mark: "After I am raised up, I will go before you to Galilee."

A quite heated discussion follows over who will and who will not desert Jesus. Peter, as usual, is right out front taking initiative, talking loudest. Peter is committed to Jesus. "All others may desert you but not I! *ouk ego!*" In words that reflect the strong form of Jesus' call to discipleship (8:34), in being willing in essence even to take up a cross for Jesus, Peter cries out, "Although I should die with you I will never deny you!" Jesus has a dire personal prediction for Peter. But note, *all* the disciples say the same.

Mark never tells us just when Judas slips away; perhaps as they leave the Passover meal, perhaps at prayer time from the garden.

> **32 They went to a place called Gethsemane; and he said to his disciples, "Sit here while I pray." 33 He took with him Peter and James and John and began to be distressed and agitated. 34 And he said to them, "I am deeply grieved, even to death; remain here, and keep awake." 35 And going a little farther, he threw himself on the ground and prayed that, if it were possible, the hour might pass from him. 36 He said, "Abba, Father, for you all things are possible; remove this cup from me; yet, not what I want, but what you want."**

"Gethsemane" is an olive oil press on this mount covered with olive trees. Jesus asks his disciples to sit by the oil press while he prays. Jesus takes three disciples a bit further, the three who climbed the mountain with him the day he was transfigured (9:2). He shares with them the agony he is experiencing. Jesus comes to pray in a state of profound inner turmoil. Expressed in strong language: he finds himself in great distress (*ekthambeisthai*), dejected and weary (*adeimonein*), surrounded by grief (*perilupos*), even unto death.

Stay here, he tells the three. Be vigilant, *greigoreite!* Keep watch!

---

4. The Greek verb involves a passive form of the verb *skandalizo*, to stumble, which the NRSV correctly translates as "become deserters." Jesus says, "You will all be caused to stumble." Peter answers, "Even if all are caused to stumble, but not I." I prefer the more direct statement, "You will desert me."

Jesus walks on a little farther, throws himself on the ground before God, and cries out, "Abba! Father!" "Abba" is the intimate Aramaic address, a child's call, "Papa." In direct address to God Jesus calls out, "Abba!"

Jesus states his own will in direct contradiction to God's will as he understands God's plan to be written in Scripture. He begs that the expected hour might pass around him, that it might be voided. He pleads, knowing and arguing that: Abba, you have the power to remove this cup. "Yet not what I will but your will be done."

I am struck by the passion and the intensity with which Jesus prays in the garden. He does not beg for halfways, for a balsam to soothe his suffering, for postponement, for six, eight, or ten more years of life, for light judgment. He goes for all or nothing. We do not find him gently kneeling next to the rock looking into the stars here. No! He throws himself on the ground, knees down, facedown to the earth perhaps, and his own will seems set in diametric opposition to God's.

But Jesus submits! He yields his life to accord with God's will.

37 He came and found them sleeping; and he said to Peter, "Simon, are you asleep? Could you not keep awake one hour? 38 Keep awake and pray that you may not come into the time of trial; the spirit indeed is willing, but the flesh is weak." 39 And again he went away and prayed, saying the same words. 40 And once more he came and found them sleeping, for their eyes were very heavy; and they did not know what to say to him.

After the first hour of intense presence before God, Jesus returns to find the three asleep. It is night. They have filled themselves on the Passover feast. Sleep is natural. Jesus chides Peter in particular, the one who most adamantly insisted on his commitment. " Could you [singular] not be vigilant one hour?" And again using the verb from the parable instructing faithful servants to be watchful, he commands the three to keep awake (*greigoreite*) and pray (plural verbs). Pray what? Pray in preparation for the time of trial. Why? Although we intend the best, human flesh is weak.

Jesus' instruction is to take a stance remarkably parallel to the one he has just taken in his own prayer. If you anticipate a difficult time ahead, if you experience inner turmoil, if you are feeling a temptation, or especially if you find yourself wanting to avoid what you understand to be God's will in your life, take time to do so honestly in the presence of your heavenly Father.

"Follow Me."

We get the impression that Jesus' hour of prayer has provided him with a certain leverage over his earlier emotions, yet he goes away to pray a second time. The disciples hear him speaking to his Abba in the same words as before. And once again Jesus submits! He yields his life to accord with God's will.

Here, as all through Mark, Jesus meets life with a certain concentrated intensity, yet his passion does not give him a narrow field of vision. He has been extraordinarily sensitive to people around him and their needs. He seems to be totally engaged in the moment, absolutely communicating with the person who is before him. We may suspect that throughout his ministry his prayers have engaged God in the same personal manner. There are structural similarities between this garden prayer and the Lord's prayer (which is not given in Mark): "Thy will be done. Thy kingdom come on earth." That is Jesus' central commitment throughout his life. And in both prayers he engages God with the very practical situations he faces: daily bread, temptation, and the suffering he has been anticipating since before the Mount of Transfiguration.

Jesus returns a second time to find the three sleeping. They know not what to say to him.

A third time Jesus leaves his disciples to converse with his heavenly Father. Of all the gospels, "Abba!" is found only in Mark 14:36. In intimate direct address Jesus again presents himself before his Abba. We might expect that he comes now more nearly ready to kneel beside the rock, looking up into heaven with complete trust, and yielding his entire life to whatever his heavenly Father has in store for him.

After a quiet time Jesus hears the occasional talk and footfalls of some group approaching.

> **41 He came a third time and said to them, "Are you still sleeping and taking your rest? Enough! The hour has come; the Son of Man is betrayed into the hands of sinners. 42 Get up, let us be going. See, my betrayer is at hand."**
> **43 Immediately, while he was still speaking, Judas, one of the twelve, arrived; and with him there was a crowd with swords and clubs, from the chief priests, the scribes, and the elders. 44 Now the betrayer had given them a sign, saying, "The one I will kiss is the man; arrest him and lead him away under guard." 45 So when he came, he went up to him at once and said, "Rabbi!" and kissed him. 46 Then they laid hands on him and arrested him. 47 But one of those who stood near drew his sword and struck the slave of the high priest, cutting off his ear. 48 Then Jesus said to**

> them, "Have you come out with swords and clubs to arrest me as though I were a bandit? 49 Day after day I was with you in the temple teaching, and you did not arrest me. But let the scriptures be fulfilled." 50 All of them deserted him and fled.

In bitter irony, Judas betrays Jesus to those who may not know him with a kiss, addressing him as "my teacher," *rabbi*. Jesus is self-possessed. He neither struggles nor resists. He confronts the crowd, verbally stating the evil they are doing. "You arrest me as a teacher by night with weapons of force as if I were a bandit? You had power to arrest me every day while I taught in the temple." Someone near Jesus draws his sword and, swinging it, cuts off a slave's ear. John tells us that was Peter's doing (John 18:10–11), but Mark does not name him.

"But let the Scriptures be fulfilled!" Along the way Jesus has taught the disciples repeatedly, in fact this very day he said that this would happen. Jesus understands that obedience puts him in the hands of sinners yet he chooses the high path laid out for him. He is persuaded that even through this betrayal and suffering he is and will be fulfilling God's will for him. In these words he lets disciples know, if only in retrospect after much more has taken place, that Jesus chooses to continue on this path with complete trust in God.

> 51 A certain young man was following him, wearing nothing but a linen cloth. They caught hold of him, 52 but he left the linen cloth and ran off naked.

The disciples get away. But there is mention of another young man who also flees. Is this, as I suspect, a vivid, self-deprecating signature by the author of the book? If so, his impression of Jesus held him in a firmer grip than the temple guards as they reached out to grab those who followed Jesus.

> 53 They took Jesus to the high priest; and all the chief priests, the elders, and the scribes were assembled. 54 Peter had followed him at a distance, right into the courtyard of the high priest; and he was sitting with the guards, warming himself at the fire. 55 Now the chief priests and the whole council were looking for testimony against Jesus to put him to death; but they found none. 56 For many gave false testimony against him, and their testimony did not agree. 57 Some stood up and gave false testimony against him, saying, 58 "We heard him say, 'I will destroy this

"Follow Me."

> temple that is made with hands, and in three days I will build another, not made with hands.'" 59 But even on this point their testimony did not agree.

Peter runs, but, probably remembering his oath, he turns back to follow the temple guards even to the chief priest's house, to the courtyard where, or near the place where, the trial takes place. Peter may observe some of the trial.

This religious trial takes place before the Sanhedrin, an assembly of scribes, elders, and chief priests under the leadership of the high priest. Given Jesus' recent confrontations in the temple, given a long-standing desire to destroy him (Mark 3:6; 11:18), it is not surprising that they seek testimony against him that would merit death. They have taken the prisoner by force before establishing the case against him. A variety of charges are made against Jesus but the testimony of witnesses does not agree. Deuteronomy 19:15 required the agreement of two or more witnesses to sustain a charge. The testimony against Jesus mentioned in Mark, that Jesus claimed that he would destroy and rebuild the temple, comes close to a claim recorded only in John 2:18–21.[5] In Mark Jesus had stated that the temple would be destroyed in what was at least a *quasi* public setting (13:1–2).

> 60 Then the high priest stood up before them and asked Jesus, "Have you no answer? What is it that they testify against you?" 61 But he was silent and did not answer. Again the high priest asked him, "Are you the Messiah, the Son of the Blessed One?" 62 Jesus said, "I am; and
>
>> 'you will see the Son of Man
>> seated at the right hand of the Power,'
>> and 'coming with the clouds of heaven.'"

Unable to get the desired testimony from others, the high priest tries to get Jesus to answer the charges. But Jesus remains silent. The high priest then asks him the direct question posed by these last days in the temple. Not, "Do you claim to be . . ." but, "Are you [second-person singular] the Messiah, the son of the Blessed One?"

---

5. When his authority for cleansing the temple was questioned, Jesus said, "Destroy this temple and in three days I will raise it up." John hastens to add that Jesus was speaking of the temple of his own body, and thus, of his resurrection. But a person in the audience could easily miss that subtle point.

Jesus' answer is most direct: "I am!" *ego eimi*. I am indeed! I am he. Only in Mark does Jesus give such a direct, emphatic answer to the high priest. And he follows this with two emphatic messianic quotes so that the point cannot be missed. Consider the quotes phrase by phrase.

Jesus takes the label he has repeatedly used to identify himself, "the Son of Man," and makes it part of his explicit claim to be God's Messiah. Jesus tells the high priest that he and the others present, "you [second person plural] shall see the Son of Man seated at the right hand of the Power." Seated "at the right hand" quotes the messianic Psalm 110:1, the conundrum verse Jesus presented to the scribes in the temple (Mark 12:35–7). "The Power" and "The Blessed One" are both common ways Jews refer to God without directly naming God. The second quote fills out the reference to Daniel (7:13–14): You will see the Son of Man "coming with the clouds of heaven . . . His dominion is an everlasting dominion that shall never pass away." It is the vision of the victorious Messiah that Jesus has already promised his disciples (13:26).

Jesus thus emphatically claims for himself the title "Christ, the son of God," with which Mark opens the book (1:1) and "the Christ" which Peter confessed in 8:29. This title is absolutely central to Jesus' self-identification for his community of followers.

What is the Messiah? Who is this Christ? Jesus is teaching us the answer even as he stands before the high priest. Mark's Gospel is a study in the meaning of God's Messiah: everything Jesus has done, the healings and forgiving, his instruction to crowds and individuals, his willingness to serve others, his acts in the temple, the acts he projects beyond the boundaries of this gospel, the example of his obedience, his willing submission to his Abba's will, his almost inexplicable crucifixion and death, his resurrection, all teach us. "I am the Christ." Is this not the mystery, the key, the secret of the kingdom his disciples were given hints of long before outsiders (4:11)?

> **63 Then the high priest tore his clothes and said, "Why do we still need witnesses? 64 You have heard his blasphemy! What is your decision?" All of them condemned him as deserving death. 65 Some began to spit on him, to blindfold him, and to strike him, saying to him, "Prophesy!" The guards also took him over and beat him.**

Why does the high priest take Jesus' claim to be God's Messiah to be blasphemous? He understands Jesus to be saying more than the common, ordinary answer to the question, "Yes, I am." Perhaps the high priest takes Jesus'

"Follow Me."

"ego eimi" to be pronouncing the absolute name for God? Most certainly Mark does not find Jesus to be misusing or abusing God's name. Very likely, however, these men were not speaking Greek but Hebrew or Aramaic. In Hebrew the words are, "I am he," *ani hu*, or, by my guess, the more emphatic *anochi hu*, "*I am* he." I expect that the high priest was ready to condemn any claim by this man from Nazareth to be the Messiah. And when Jesus emphatically adds that God will reward him with a seat at God's right hand he might question whether Jesus nearly elevates himself to a level with God.

It is a moment of intense emotion for the high priest. "Blasphemy!" he cries, tearing his garments with the gesture prescribed as a response to blasphemy. It is a serious charge. Leviticus 24:16 states, "One who blasphemes the name of the Lord shall be put to death. The whole congregation shall stone the blasphemer."[6] If the high priest's judgment is correct, Jesus deserves to die by the Law of Moses. And the council present with the high priest, says Mark, all condemn Jesus to die.

We too are invited to pass judgment. Is this Jesus the true Messiah? And the companion question implied by those who later taunt Jesus from the foot of the cross may haunt us as well: Can a man God allows to be crucified be God's Anointed?

> **66 While Peter was below in the courtyard, one of the servant-girls of the high priest came by. 67 When she saw Peter warming himself, she stared at him and said, "You also were with Jesus, the man from Nazareth." 68 But he denied it, saying, "I do not know or understand what you are talking about." And he went out onto the forecourt. Then the cock crowed. 69 And the servant girl, on seeing him, began again to say to the bystanders, "This man is one of them." 70 But again he denied it. Then after a little while the bystanders again said to Peter, "Certainly you are one of them; for you are a Galilean." 71 But he began to curse, and he swore an oath, "I do not know this man you are talking about." 72 At that moment the cock crowed for the second time. Then Peter remembered that Jesus had said to him, "Before the cock crows twice, you will deny me three times." And he broke down and wept.**

---

6. The strict interpretation of blasphemy would be that a person is "not guilty unless he pronounces the Name." The basic meaning of the Greek word "blaspheme" is "to abuse, to insult." There is no reason to think that any of the Gospel writers thought that Jesus was misusing the name of God. Brown, *Death of the Messiah*, 520–52.

Mark Chapter 14

Between the religious and civil trials of Jesus, Mark tells of a trial that Peter experiences. In the courtyard of the high priest, no less, Peter is indeed doing what he can to follow Jesus, given the circumstances. But he finds himself in a precarious spot. The conversation veers occasionally to the entrapment in the garden, what is transpiring inside, or who this Jesus is. A servant girl recognizes Peter. Perhaps she had seen Peter with Jesus in the temple, if not that very night. "You were with Jesus," the servant says, "You are one of them, a disciple." Others join in against Peter, "You certainly are one of them! Your accent gives you away. You're from Galilee."

Peter has grounds to be concerned for his own personal safety, given Jesus' fix. But the context includes another danger. The council is actively seeking testimony against Jesus to put Jesus to death. If the council can get a match of two testimonies the case is made. Who better to corroborate somebody's testimony than one of the disciples?

Peter denies it twice. The third time he curses and swears a strong oath. "I do not know [*ouk oida*] this man you speak of." The cock crows a second time. Peter hears. At once he remembers what this man said, the one he has just cursed over. He rushes out to weep in great grief.

There is painful irony in Peter's swearing he does not know Jesus, to whom Peter is—I do not doubt it even here—deeply committed. Note also how deeply ironic are the quoted claims by Jesus' opponents, given Mark's presupposition. The high priest and all the council condemn Jesus to death as, in the high priest's words, "The Messiah, the Son of the Blessed One," a phrase whose other occurrence is in Mark's opening words (Mark 1:1). The guards taunt a blindfolded Jesus, "Play the prophet! Tell us! Who struck you?" while at that moment Jesus' words to Peter about the cock crow are fulfilled in the courtyard.

I am struck by the repeated juxtapositions of the commands to watch (*blepete*), to keep awake (*greigoreite*) and to pray on the one hand, and the capacity to see, to perceive, and to know (*oida*) on the other, found in this section of Mark. What can we learn from this? The earlier acts are evidently meant to be a kind of preparation for the latter. At the end of the last chapter disciples are instructed to keep awake for we do not know the hour when we must be ready (Mark 13:35–37). In the garden three disciples are instructed to keep awake, once again, and to pray, to be ready. When Jesus finds them sleeping they do not know what to say (14:40). Now, caught between a rock and a hard place, Peter can only insist that he does not know.

Mark Chapter 15

15 As soon as it was morning, the chief priests held a consultation with the elders and scribes and the whole council. They bound Jesus, led him away, and handed him over to Pilate. 2 Pilate asked him, "Are you the King of the Jews?" He answered him, "You say so." 3 Then the chief priests accused him of many things. 4 Pilate asked him again, "Have you no answer? See how many charges they bring against you." 5 But Jesus made no further reply, so that Pilate was amazed.

THE CHIEF PRIESTS HAVE another consultation with the whole council, the Sanhedrin, early in the morning. They had reached a judgment against Jesus the night before. Now they make preparations to carry it out. They bind Jesus and turn him over to Pilate with an accusation that involves Jesus claiming to be the King of the Jews.

A subtle rubbing between cultures can be seen in the present exchanges. The Roman procurator, Pilate, cares nothing for a Jewish messiah as long as he holds no threat to Rome. And blasphemy, the charge on which the Sanhedrin judged Jesus guilty, is a religious matter that Pilate would leave to the Jews. Those charges will get nowhere. Pilate will insist on exerting Roman political might over the Jews but would want to prevent a riot, especially when the city is so crowded for Passover. Now, many Jews hoped that the Messiah, a descendant of King David, would rule as king and free them from the military oppression they were suffering under Rome. Hadn't Jesus accepted the title of king of Israel when he rode into Jerusalem? Further, he has claimed positively before the high priest that he is the Messiah. "King of the Jews" would provide the rough equivalent term for outsiders, with an

MARK CHAPTER 15

emphasis on the usual political and military dimensions of kingship. Now, sedition against Rome would be a political charge that Pilate must address. If the religious leaders can sustain that charge, Pilate must listen to them.

But Jesus has not taken up arms against Caesar. "What wrong has he done to merit death?" Pilate would ask, as we hear him ask the crowd later (Mark 15:14). The priests persist. So Pilate asks Jesus directly:

"Are you the King of the Jews?"

"You say so," Jesus answers.

This is certainly not the emphatic answer Jesus had for the high priest. But neither is Pilate's question the same sort of question the high priest asked. It comes out in political terms, the sort of terms that Herod Antipas, for instance, would be decidedly interested in. Jesus does not deny it. There is an important sense in which he projects becoming king, the servant king in his Father's kingdom in the age to come, but he avoids the immediate political and military overtones involved in Pilate's question. Given the circumstances, I see his answer as a subtle but strong affirmative, a conscious expression of the alternative Messiah that Jesus has chosen to become perhaps as early as his desert sojourn after his baptism and which we have witnessed in the remainder of Mark's Gospel.

Getting so little at this point, the chief priests go on to accuse Jesus before Pilate of many other things. Jesus does not answer those charges. Pilate recognizes that the priests find Jesus a threat and want to be rid of him (15:10), and he must understand that they want him, Pilate, to carry out that task for them. Yet Jesus does not even try to defend himself. "Have you no reply?" Pilate asks in amazement. Jesus simply stands, silent.

> **6 Now at the festival he used to release a prisoner for them, anyone for whom they asked. 7 Now a man called Barabbas was in prison with the rebels who had committed murder during the insurrection. 8 So the crowd came and began to ask Pilate to do for them according to his custom. 9 Then he answered them, "Do you want me to release for you the King of the Jews?" 10 For he realized that it was out of jealousy that the chief priests had handed him over. 11 But the chief priests stirred up the crowd to have him release Barabbas for them instead. 12 Pilate spoke to them again, "Then what do you wish me to do with the man you call the King of the Jews?" 13 They shouted back, "Crucify him!" 14 Pilate asked them, "Why? What evil has he done?" But they shouted all the more, "Crucify him!" 15 So Pilate, wishing**

"Follow Me."

> **to satisfy the crowd, released Barabbas for them; and after flogging Jesus, he handed him over to be crucified.**

Barabbas is a popular insurrectionist. In Aramaic "Barabbas" means literally "son of a father." We thus get a play on the names, for God twice called Jesus "Son" in Mark (1:11; 9:7), and Jesus calls God "Abba" (14:36). Pilate presents the crowd a choice between these two sons. "King of the Jews," a title that Pilate used first, perhaps in disbelief, disdain, or even mirth, he uses twice before the crowd, taunting the chief priests.

The crowd will not be talked out of the man they want freed this holiday. "Give us Barabbas! Crucify the other fellow!" Pilate has Jesus flogged, and hands him over to the Roman soldiers to be crucified.

The structure of the two trials, religious and political, are parallel in several respects. In both trials the majority of charges brought against Jesus are suspect. Each trial ends in abuse of Jesus. After each trial there is a further consultation about what to do. Throughout this ordeal we note Jesus' quiet dignity, the self-possession of a man submitting to a larger cause in obedience to his understanding of his heavenly Father's will. In both trials the one question Jesus answers is the crucial charge against him. Mark plays the irony against the accusers. Jesus affirms the accusers' words. Jesus claims the title knowing he will die for it. "I am God's Messiah," and in a more subtle way, "I am a king." It is the single truth that matters!

> **16 Then the soldiers led him into the courtyard of the palace (that is, the governor's headquarters); and they called together the whole cohort. 17 And they clothed him in a purple cloak; and after twisting some thorns into a crown, they put it on him. 18 And they began saluting him, "Hail, King of the Jews!" 19 They struck his head with a reed, spat upon him, and knelt down in homage to him. 20 After mocking him, they stripped him of the purple cloak and put his own clothes on him. Then they led him out to crucify him.**

The soldiers mock Jesus in their own coarse drama. They strip Jesus, throw a cloth of purple over his shoulders, weave thorns into a mock laurel wreath, and crown him. The cohort is called to join in to witness the coronation. Spitting in his face, striking him with a reed, they kneel to do him homage. And again, with Mark's irony, mock him, "Hail! King of the Jews!" They assert their power over this man by stripping him again. They fling his own garment over him and lead him out to be crucified.

> 21 They compelled a passer-by, who was coming in from the country, to carry his cross; it was Simon of Cyrene, the father of Alexander and Rufus. 22 Then they brought Jesus to the place called Golgotha (which means the place of a skull). 23 And they offered him wine mixed with myrrh; but he did not take it. 24 And they crucified him, and divided his clothes among them, casting lots to decide what each should take.
> 25 It was nine o'clock in the morning when they crucified him. 26 The inscription of the charge against him read, "The King of the Jews." 27 And with him they crucified two bandits, one on his right and one on his left.

Simon of Cyrene is forcibly recruited to carry Jesus' cross along the way. Evidently Mark expects his readers to know this Simon and his two sons. Perhaps Simon took an interest in this man whose cross he bore on his shoulders, and later joined a community of persons seeking to follow Jesus with his two sons. Rome used the painful and humiliating death by crucifixion to deal with political rebels, revolutionaries, and bandits. From Rome's vantage the cross was a public display of triumph over enemies of the state. Jesus was not an enemy of the state.

At Golgotha the soldiers offer Jesus wine mixed with myrrh to assuage the physical agony of crucifixion. Jesus refuses it. They crucify Jesus and raise up his cross. The soldiers cast lots for his garment, an act that echoes Psalm 22:18. Three times in this crucifixion narrative, events that take place echo the words of Psalm 22. This psalm expresses the cry in first-person singular of someone in the throes of great suffering who still hopes for God's deliverance. Two bandits are crucified with Jesus, in positions requested by James and John.

An inscription is written and posted above his head so that onlookers may know his crime: "The King of the Jews." This is the fifth time in this chapter that Rome used this title for Jesus.

> 29 Those who passed by derided him, shaking their heads and saying, "Aha! You who would destroy the temple and build it in three days, 30 save yourself, and come down from the cross!" 31 In the same way the chief priests, along with the scribes, were also mocking him among themselves and saying, "He saved others; he cannot save himself. 32

"Follow Me."

> Let the Messiah, the King of Israel, come down from the cross now, so that we may see and believe." Those who were crucified with him also taunted him.

We now get a procession of people who make it a point to continue to mock Jesus. "All who see me mock at me, they make mouths at me, they wag their heads," says Psalm 22:7 (RSV). Passersby do just that. Testimony from the high priest's trial about a temple claim is repeated as a jeer from the foot of the cross. The scribes and priests join the taunting, and with Mark's irony say, "He saved others. But look, he cannot save himself." They scorn him, using the insider's phrases for the charge inscribed above his head. "Climb down off your cross. *Then* we will believe that you are the Messiah, and King of Israel." Even the bandits join in the mockery.

What if Mark's account should end here, at the lowest point in Jesus' ministry? It looks like the taunters have managed to bring about a total defeat of this man. Would Mark have called it good news? Would we call this book a gospel? This gospel presents a particular challenge to us because Mark will not give us trumpet-blaring triumphs. But even at this moment there is irony. It is precisely in refusing to save himself that Jesus has obeyed his Abba's will, to redeem and to save others. Even as Jesus hangs dying on the cross, he fulfills what he told his disciples bluntly three times that the Messiah must face in Jerusalem.

Why must it come to this? There is a disturbing mystery here that Mark rightfully leaves as mystery. We must remind ourselves that this is a portion of God's way of handling things that we may not understand. And what does it accomplish? Mark's Jesus says very little in direct answer to that question. He told his disciples that he came to preach the good news that the kingdom of God is near at hand, "Repent and believe the good news!" (Mark 1:14-15, 38). He claimed authority on earth to forgive sins (2:5, 10). In some instructions to his disciples on how to follow him, Jesus said, "I have come to serve and to give my life as a ransom for many" (10:45). At the Last Supper, at their Passover meal, in a free act Jesus broke the bread and gave it to his disciples saying, "Take, this is my body." And passing the cup of wine around he told them, "This is my blood of the covenant which is poured out for many" (14:22-24). Mark's Jesus has acted freely, choosing at every step God's way of unrelenting love. Must a true, freeing, serving love involve such suffering as this in its encounter with human shortsightedness and evil? That is what we have witnessed. But if Jesus has emphasized that he must die in Jerusalem, the disciples will remember that he told them just as emphatically that after three days he would rise again. Given the fact that the resurrection is part of Mark's story, it seems clear that Mark understands what takes place on the cross to be a crucial portion of God's redemptive action in our world. But he does not try to explain how this act of unrelenting love redeems us or the world. Perhaps the best human response is to be found in choosing to live a humble life promoting justice and mercy even as we fall far short of full understanding.

> **33 When it was noon, darkness came over the whole land until three in the afternoon. 34 At three o'clock Jesus cried out with a loud voice, "Eloi, Eloi, lema sabachthani?" which means, "My God, my God, why have you forsaken me?" 35 When some of the bystanders heard it, they said, "Listen, he is calling for Elijah." 36 And someone ran, filled a sponge with sour wine, put it on a stick, and gave it to him to drink, saying, "Wait, let us see whether Elijah will come to take him down." 37 Then Jesus gave a loud cry and breathed his last. 38 And the curtain of the temple was torn in two, from top to bottom. 39 Now when the centurion, who stood facing him, saw that in this way he breathed his last, he said, "Truly this man was God's son!"**

Three hours of mockery after the crucifixion are followed by three hours of darkness over the land. The sun hidden from sight at midday provides an omen, a visible, if minimal, physical manifestation of God's judgment. Throughout his crucifixion, Mark's Jesus suffers in silence. Toward the end of the darkness Jesus cries out with a great voice.

"*Eloi, Eloi, lema sabachthani?*" is transliterated into Greek from the Aramaic rather than the Hebrew version of Psalm 22:1. Like his address to God in the garden, Jesus cries out in Aramaic, the tongue he commonly spoke growing up. Although the psalm ends in God's victory, the agony of this moment comes out in the psalm's first words. Not addressing God as Father, not with the intimate Abba, but for the first time in the Gospel we hear Jesus using the more distant *Eloi*, "My God." It is the cry of anguish out of suffering. Jesus does not doubt God's existence. He cries "*Eloi!*" He cries, "My God. Why?" With the psalmist's human agony he asks, "Why have you, my God, forsaken me?" There is but silence. Silence. No voice is heard in answer.

"Follow Me."

A bystander misinterprets "Eloi" as a cry for Elijah. The person in charge of the sponge rushes to fill the sponge with wine to lift it to Jesus' lips, and then waits to see if Elijah will somehow come to rescue Jesus.

Letting out a second loud cry, Jesus breathes his last breath and dies. And in a second physical omen not far distant, but not visible from Golgotha, the temple curtain is torn from top to bottom. The temple has not won! This curtain torn in two is described with the same verb Mark used to portray the heavens tearing open when God first spoke to Jesus in an audible voice (1:10).

After Jesus' loud cry, last breath, and death, we begin to encounter a series of responses to his death. First is a centurion, the leader in charge of a hundred soldiers and responsible for this crucifixion, who must have witnessed what we have witnessed and conversed with various members of the crowd. The centurion was impressed on seeing how Jesus met his death. He exclaimed, "Truly [using the Greek word *aleithos* rather than the Hebrew *Amen*] this man was a son of God." Some people argue that the centurion is the first convert after Jesus' death, confessing that Jesus is the Son of God. Perhaps. However, Mark's Greek has no definite article here to make it "*the* Son of God." On the other hand, the Greek phrase "Jesus Christ, Son of God" of Mark 1:1 has no definite article either. More likely, in another Markan irony, this centurion speaks a greater truth than he comprehends.

> **40 There were also women looking on from a distance; among them were Mary Magdalene, and Mary the mother of James the younger and of Joses, and Salome. 41 These used to follow him and provided for him when he was in Galilee; and there were many other women who had come up with him to Jerusalem.**

We are now told that women, followers of Jesus, have been standing as onlookers near the cross. They have hardly been mentioned in Mark's story. These women are disciples who have served Jesus, who provided (*diekonoun*) for him and his followers in Galilee.

These women have followed and ministered to Jesus since the early days. Mark used this same verb to describe Peter's mother-in-law who jumped out of bed to *serve* them (1:31). These are the quiet followers, the hidden ones who have served faithfully along the way. They have followed Jesus' instruction and example perhaps more faithfully than the twelve. When the dozen vied over who should get most acclaim, Jesus used the servant verb to describe himself: "The Son of Man has come not to be served to but to serve, and to give his life as a ransom for many" (10:45). These women are not in hiding. From among the greater number of women standing nearby, three in particular are singled out by name: Mary Magdalene, Salome, and Mary the mother of James the younger and Joses. The people of Nazareth used a similar phrase in describing Mary the mother of Jesus (6:3).

> 42 When evening had come, and since it was the day of Preparation, that is, the day before the sabbath, 43 Joseph of Arimathea, a respected member of the council, who was also himself waiting expectantly for the kingdom of God, went boldly to Pilate and asked for the body of Jesus. 44 Then Pilate wondered if he were already dead; and summoning the centurion, he asked him whether he had been dead for some time. 45 When he learned from the centurion that he was dead, he granted the body to Joseph. 46 Then Joseph bought a linen cloth, and taking down the body, wrapped it in the linen cloth, and laid it in a tomb that had been hewn out of the rock. He then rolled a stone against the door of the tomb. 47 Mary Magdalene and Mary the mother of Joses saw where the body was laid.

The preparation for burial is hasty. Jesus died at three in the afternoon. Joseph of Arimathea, a member of the council, is anxious to have Jesus in the tomb before sunset, the beginning of Sabbath. He has had to wait to get an audience with Pilate. Joseph requests that he be given Jesus' body for burial. Pilate summons the centurion. They wait until the centurion comes in. The centurion, most likely the one we found in charge of Jesus' crucifixion, testifies that Jesus has been dead for some time. Joseph buys new linen in which to wrap the body. The body is removed from the cross and placed in a tomb. The two Marys still at the cross follow him and observe where Jesus is laid. A stone is rolled against the door of the tomb. There is not enough time to purchase and then to anoint Jesus' body with aromatic oils.

Joseph of Arimathea performs an important service for Jesus, whatever his motives. He may be attending to a point of ritual purity on behalf on the Sanhedrin (Deut 21:22–23). On the other hand, as one waiting expectantly for the kingdom of God, he may have been sympathetic to Jesus' teachings or even a hidden follower, for the kingdom of God was central to Jesus' ministry.

Mark Chapter 16

16 When the sabbath was over, Mary Magdalene, and Mary the mother of James, and Salome bought spices, so that they might go and anoint him. 2 And very early on the first day of the week, when the sun had risen, they went to the tomb. 3 They had been saying to one another, "Who will roll away the stone for us from the entrance to the tomb?" 4 When they looked up, they saw that the stone, which was very large, had already been rolled back. 5 As they entered the tomb, they saw a young man, dressed in a white robe, sitting on the right side; and they were alarmed. 6 But he said to them, "Do not be alarmed; you are looking for Jesus of Nazareth, who was crucified. He has been raised; he is not here. Look, there is the place they laid him. 7 But go, tell his disciples and Peter that he is going ahead of you to Galilee; there you will see him, just as he told you."

AT SUNRISE AFTER SABBATH, the two Marys and Salome bring aromatic spices to the tomb to anoint Jesus' body and to minister to him a last time, wondering how they can move the heavy stone that blocks the entry. When they arrive, the tomb is open!

They enter the open tomb and see a young man in *leukein*, white or bright, apparel. The same adjective was used to describe Jesus' transfiguration garment (Mark 9:3). The young man is seated near the spot where the two Marys saw Jesus' body placed on Sabbath eve. The women are astonished. "Do not be alarmed," the young man tells them.

"Jesus is not here." He identifies Jesus as the man from Nazareth whom they saw crucified and points out where Jesus was placed. "Jesus has been raised up!" His words will become a confessional formula for the early church: "Jesus, who was crucified, is risen from the dead!"

And he instructs them to go tell the disciples, and Peter in particular, that "Jesus goes ahead of you to Galilee. You will see him there, just as he told you."

8 So they went out and fled from the tomb, for terror and amazement had seized them; and they said nothing to anyone, for they were afraid.

The women are suddenly overcome with feeling. They flee from the tomb swept by intense, even contradictory, emotions. Out of their minds with terror and bewilderment, or with fearful trembling mixed with ecstasy, depending on how we translate the two nouns (*tromos* and *ekstasis*),[1] the women falter. Fright, mixed with an overwhelming joy over the mystery of the risen Jesus! They must catch their breath. For now, we are told, they speak to no one because they are afraid.

How can Mark's Gospel end here? Verse 8 is in fact the end of the most ancient and reliable texts of Mark we have. Why does Mark end this story as the women falter? These three women, who have done the hidden servant's work from the beginning, who followed Jesus to Jerusalem, to the cross, to his burial site, and who have come to complete the preparation for his burial, are left at a moment of stumbling. Even these, the most faithful of his followers, fall in fright.

And, as if to accentuate the fear experienced at the tomb, Mark ends his Greek text with the conjunction, *gar*, which means "because" or "indeed." How do you end a text with a conjunction? The two last words are *ephobounto gar*. The thought that these disciples were frightened is put as an exclamation. They were afraid indeed!

This fear is part of Mark's realism in dealing with disciples. It leaves us open to our human vulnerabilities. We want to finish this story. The postscript shares some of my grappling with this ending. It simply cannot end here. Mark leaves us amidst a human misstep.

We turn to the tomb to consider what has just happened, once again. The young man's instruction is to go to Galilee. That act can provide a focus for the disciples who have scattered and have become disoriented at their

---

1. Remember the girl's parents' ecstasy in Mark's previous use of the second noun (5:42).

"Follow Me."

Messiah's death. The words beckon to familiar territory. It is a final invitation in Mark to follow Jesus.

Jesus is risen! Much of what Jesus foretold has already been fulfilled in precise detail. And there are promises Jesus made that reach beyond this moment, like the subtle forward look to Galilee (14:28) or the vision of God's kingdom come in its glory (13:26). There is the example of Jesus' constant trust that the Father's will is good.

Out of the tomb again we rush. Mark catches us mid-stride. I too have faltered. I have said nothing. We are left to pick ourselves up with the women to finish the story. The words invite us to begin the story anew in Galilee, to return to the opening chapters of Mark or, opening to the chapters of our lives, learn what it can mean for us. "He goes ahead of you." Will you follow?

Postscript

MANY READERS, MYSELF INCLUDED, find the original ending of Mark disconcerting. We would like Mark to tell more about what happens after this moment at the tomb, to tell when the disciples hear the news, what they do, what happens when they meet Jesus in Galilee, and so forth. This very response may have driven Matthew and Luke and John to write their Gospels because in each of their accounts the women tell the disciples what they have just experienced, and they each fill out the story with at least two resurrection encounters with Jesus.

Taken together we are told of numerous encounters with the risen Christ. Matthew speaks of Jesus meeting two Marys and his commissioning the eleven disciples at their meeting in Galilee (Matt 28:1, 8–10,16–20). In John's account Jesus appears to Mary Magdalene, and he appears twice to the disciples (with Thomas present the second time). John ends his book with a fourth encounter; Jesus meets Peter and six other disciples at the Sea of Galilee (John 20:11–29; 21:1–23). Luke tells us that Jesus walked with Cleopas and another disciple on the road to Emmaus and spoke to them concerning all the biblical passages related to his death and resurrection. Jesus went through the lesson again when he showed his hands and feet to his disciples later that night. Luke mentions Jesus' ascent into heaven (Luke 24:13–53). The book of Acts mentions forty days of instructions and, again, the ascension (Acts 1:1–11). The disciples were convinced that Jesus is *the* Messiah. On the day of Pentecost (Acts 2) and repeatedly thereafter, Peter preached with confidence that "Jesus of Nazareth [who was] crucified and killed . . . this Jesus God raised up, and of that all of us are witnesses. Know with certainty that God has made him both Lord and Messiah" (Acts 2:22–24, 32, 36). It is an astonishing claim for a Jew to make, given the Messiah expected by the Jews. Yet every book of the New Testament proclaims that Jesus is the Messiah.[1]

Now back to Mark's ending. Every author has to choose where to begin, and where to end. We should recognize, however, that Mark has a very Christian ending. He did not end with Jesus on the cross or with his burial, which would have emphasized Jesus' ministry and death. He ends with an open tomb, with a resurrected Messiah, with a messenger who tells the followers who first come to the tomb that Jesus has indeed been raised from the dead. He reminds the women of Jesus' words, which provide a context to this death and resurrection. Jesus told you he was going up to Jerusalem to die, that this was his task as Messiah, and that he would be raised from the dead in three days. Now Jesus goes before you to Galilee just as he told you. Go and meet him there. Trust God. Do not fear.

The short ending of Mark can speak powerfully to us. It points to the resurrected Christ but it does not attempt to bolster the claim with evidence beyond the empty tomb and the young man's claim. It does not try to make it appear more reasonable than it is. Mark is comfortable leaving us in the midst of our questions and faltering even while he invites us to have faith, to accept the good news, and to follow Jesus.

The empty tomb, the resurrection of Jesus, is an extraordinary event. What are we to think about it? That is one of the oldest important questions in the history of Christianity. I can only suggest a place to begin. The resurrection of Jesus is at least God's powerful affirmation of Jesus' life and ministry and of his final act of obedience. This goes beyond the claim that what Jesus foretold about his encounters in Jerusalem, his death and being raised from out of death, was affirmed in what happened. It affirms that the title Jesus accepted from his disciples, which he claimed before the high priest and Pilate, is correct, that Jesus is God's Messiah, the man anointed with God's spirit. It affirms that Jesus is the king of Israel, the servant king who will reign with power in God's kingdom come.

If Jesus is God's Messiah, he spoke true when he said that the kingdom of God is at hand; he reached out to sinners, to people who falter, to outcasts, to children, to the least pauper in human kingdoms, and welcomed us and lifted us up as children of God. If Jesus is filled with God's spirit, his work of healing the physical body and forgiving and restoring the human spirit is God's work on earth; and the acts of power, which we may not understand any more than did the disciples present when they occurred,

---

1. Dahl, "Crucified Messiah," 24.

Postscript

are signs of God's power on earth. If Jesus is Messiah, his stern reproaches against excesses practiced in the name of Moses' Law must be listened to, as must his teaching that what God commands us can be found in the books of Moses: that the Lord our God is one; that we are called to love God with everything, with all of heart, all of soul, all of strength, all of mind, and commanded to love our neighbors as we love ourselves. We are invited to *do* this and live! If Jesus is the Messiah, the gifts of the kingdom of God are indeed available to those who would follow him in this present age, despite persecution; we can trust that we will find life in abundance in God's presence when the kingdom of God comes to its fullness in the age to come.

Jesus invites us to follow him. Where does his path take us? His way involves listening for and then obeying the will of God in this life, acting with what God presents at each turn. He seeks to free each of us from slavery to ourselves. He teaches his followers that in giving one's life to others in love, a person finds the true meaning, the essential value, of life. He calls the ill-defined community of his followers to serve others, starting with the smallest child. Is this a dour existence? I think not. Jesus set out seeking a true justice filled with love. Jesus enjoys a good party with wine. He must be tickled, most pleased, when he feeds five thousand from two fish and five loaves! He may have a twinkle in his eye as he buys time to think in a hot exchange, "Show me the coin you pay your taxes with."

Recall the first words of Mark. This book is meant to be the *beginning* of the good news of Jesus Christ the son of God. The good news of Jesus Christ continues where Mark leaves off. As I see it, our most important task is not to try to explain miracles to the intellect. It is to explore what it means in our own lives to follow Jesus and to allow the mystery of God's Spirit to breathe through us as well.

Songs of the Servant of Yahweh

WHAT OF THE SONGS of the Servant of Yahweh suggested by the voice from heaven at Jesus' baptism? The songs are a modern title for four poetic segments in Isaiah that explicitly mention the servant of Yahweh. That Jesus was familiar with Isaiah is shown not only by Jesus' direct quotations of Isaiah in Mark (Mark 4:12; 7:6–7; and 11:17) but also by two episodes not mentioned in Mark. Luke 4:16–21 states that when Jesus came to Nazareth he unrolled the Isaiah scroll to a text closely related to the songs of the servant (our chapter 61) and read the passage that begins, "The Spirit of the Lord has been given to me, for he has anointed me. He has sent me to bring the good news to the poor," and Jesus claimed, "This text is being fulfilled today even as you listen" (JB). A second episode is found in Matthew 11:2–6 and Luke 7:18–23. John the Baptist wondered if he had understood matters correctly at the time of Jesus' baptism. John sent a message from prison to ask Jesus, "Are you the one who is to come, or have we got to wait for someone else?" Are you the Messiah? Jesus answers with words that allude to Isaiah: "Go back and tell John what you have seen and heard: the blind see again, the lame walk, lepers are cleansed, and the deaf hear, the dead are raised to life, the Good News is proclaimed to the poor, and happy is the man who does not lose faith in me" (Luke 7:22, JB). The allusions are to Isaiah 26:19; 29:18–19; 35:5–6; and 61:1.

We have no proof that Jesus took the four songs of the servant as a general model for the Messiah he would become. On the other hand, they do present a rather coherent portrait for such a servant, and in retrospect the pattern fits the evidence of his life. Further, in the book of Acts both Peter (Acts 3:13, 26) and the apostolic community (4:27, 30) characterize Jesus as God's servant. And Phillip, one of the twelve disciples, has no hesitation in applying the suffering servant passage of Isaiah 53 to Jesus (Acts 8:26–39).

Songs of the Servant of Yahweh

Isaiah wrote to the Jews in exile in Babylon (Isa 40–55) to console them, calling them to make a highway through the desert back to Jerusalem where they would again gather as God's people (Isa 40:1-11). This provides the context within which four songs that make a direct mention of the servant of God are written. Who is this servant? Sometimes called Israel (49:3), sometimes it is a person who is to bring Israel home (49:6); the servant will become a light extending the offer of justice (42:4) and salvation (49:6) to all people.

Certain qualifications should be kept in mind as we consider these songs. The Jewish tradition of Jesus' day did not treat these songs as a unit; the phrase "servant of God" was not considered a distinct title, it does not necessarily designate a single person, nor was it customarily understood to refer to the Messiah. There is "no indication" that "the Messiah was expected to suffer after installation to office or that his suffering was viewed as atoning in light of Isaiah 53," before Jesus lived his extraordinary life.[1] Isaiah probably did not understand these passages in the way that I suggest that Jesus came to read them. But the words heard from heaven at his baptism, "in whom I am well pleased," are enough to draw Jesus' attention to these songs. Jesus gleaned a different lesson from the songs of the servant of Yahweh than did his contemporaries.

I suggest that Jesus knew these passages well, and that in conjunction with the background of Isaiah's Davidic king who rules with integrity, justice, mercy and healing, the servant songs draw a unifying portrait that helped form Jesus' understanding of God's will for him. This portrait is summarized in the words that Jesus read aloud from Isaiah 61 and applied publicly to himself at the synagogue in Nazareth (Luke 4:16-21). And when we look at the gospel records of Jesus' ministry, his interactions with sinners, with the weak, the ill, the poor, and his obedience unto death, I would say that Jesus consciously chose to live and to give his life in a manner that embodied the spirit of Isaiah's songs, to become a servant king rather than the conquering king of Psalm 2:9.

I will use *The Jerusalem Bible*'s translation of these songs. "Yahweh" is believed to reflect an ancient pronunciation of God's name given to Moses at the burning bush, Exodus 3:14. The NRSV replaces "Yahweh" with "the LORD" (small capitals), where the Jews will say "*Adonai*." It is good to

---

1. Juel, *Messianic Exegesis*, 121-27, provides evidence for each of these negative claims about Jewish tradition. On page 127 Juel asserts the final, quoted claim as being true "prior to Christianity," not "before Jesus" as I have put it.

know how to be able to identify and to respect the God of whom we speak or address. I break each of the songs of the servant of Yahweh where the *Jerusalem Bible* does, but I use my own labels: "Song," and "Reflection"—a response that does not merely echo but reflects upon what came before.

First Song of the Servant of Yahweh (Isaiah 42:1–8)

Song:

1 "Here is my servant whom I uphold,
   my chosen one in whom my soul delights.
   I have endowed him with my spirit
   that he may bring true justice to the nations.

2 He does not cry out or shout aloud,
   or make his voice heard in the streets.
3 He does not break the crushed reed,
   nor quench the wavering flame.

   Faithfully he brings true justice;
4 he will neither waiver, nor be crushed
   until true justice is established on earth,
   for the islands are awaiting his law."

Reflection:

5 Thus says God, Yahweh,
   he who created the heavens and spread them out,
   who gave shape to the earth and what comes from it,
   who gave breath to its people
   and life to the creatures that move in it:

6 "I, Yahweh, have called you to serve the cause of right;
   I have taken you by the hand and formed you;
   I have appointed you as covenant of the people and light of the nations,

7		to open the eyes of the blind,
		to free captives from prison,
		and those who live in darkness from the dungeon.
8		My name is Yahweh,
		I will not yield my glory to another."

The first song is spoken as God's address to the servant filled with God's spirit so that he may bring justice to the nations. It characterizes the way this servant is to go about his task and affirms a final victory. The reflection identifies God, Yahweh, as the One who calls the servant and provides certain details reminiscent of earlier Isaiah passages concerning the Davidic king's task.[2]

Second Song of the Servant of Yahweh (Isaiah 49:1–9)

Song:

1   Islands, listen to me,
pay attention, remotest peoples.
Yahweh called me before I was born,
from my mother's womb he pronounced my name.

2   He made my mouth a sharp sword,
and hid me in the shadow of his hand.
He made me into a sharpened arrow,
and concealed me in his quiver.

3   He said to me, 'You are my servant Israel
in whom I shall be glorified';
4   while I was thinking, 'I have toiled in vain,

---

2. These themes are certainly not unique to the servant songs. The first song contains lines that are like those in passages from Isaiah 11:1–5, 10, while the reflection contains lines like those from Isaiah 35:5–6 and from chapter 29, that in the Day of the Lord:
"In a short time . . . the deaf, that day,
will hear the words of a book, and . . .
the eyes of the blind will see.
But the lowly will rejoice in Yahweh even more
and the poorest exult in the Holy One of Israel." (Isa 29:17–19, JB)

"Follow Me."

        I have exhausted myself for nothing';

        and all the while my cause was with Yahweh,
        my reward with my God.

5b   I was honored in the eyes of Yahweh,
        my God was my strength.

5a   And now Yahweh has spoken,
        he who formed me in the womb to be his servant,
        to bring Jacob back to him,
        to gather Israel to him:

6   'It is not enough for you to be my servant,
        to restore the tribes of Jacob and bring back the survivors of Israel;
        I will make you the light of the nations
        so that my salvation may reach to the ends of the earth.'

Reflection:

7   Thus says Yahweh,
        the redeemer of Israel and his Holy One,
        to him whose life is despised, whom the nations loathe,
        to the slave of despots:
        Kings will stand up when they see you,
        and princes will bow,
        for the sake of Yahweh who has been faithful,
        the Holy One of Israel who has chosen you.

8   Thus says Yahweh:
        At the favorable time I will answer you,
        on the day of salvation I will help you.
        I have formed you and have appointed you
        as covenant of the people.
        I will restore the land
        and assign you the estates that lie waste.

9   I will say to the prisoners, 'Come out,'
        to those who are in darkness, 'Show yourselves.'

The second song is spoken as the servant's response to God's call. The servant exults in the fact that he is created to be God's hidden sharp instrument, called to glorify God even while he believed he had toiled in vain. Indeed the servant honored God before he knew his full task: to become a light to the nations! In the reflection God affirms the servant (along with the first hint that humans despise the servant), to honor him and to make him a covenant of the people.

Third Song of the Servant of Yahweh (Isaiah 50:4–11)

Song:

4 The Lord Yahweh has given me
a disciple's tongue.
So that I may know how to reply to the wearied
he provides me with speech.
Each morning he wakes me to hear,
to listen like a disciple.
The Lord Yahweh has opened my ear.

5 For my part, I made no resistance,
neither did I turn away.
6 I offered my back to those who struck me,
my cheeks to those who tore at my beard;
I did not cover my face
against insult and spittle.

7 The Lord Yahweh comes to my help,
so that I am untouched by the insults.
So, too, I set my face like flint;
I know I shall not be shamed.

8 My vindicator is here at hand. Does anyone start proceedings against me?
Then let us go to court together.
Who thinks he has a case against me?
Let him approach me.

"Follow Me."

9   The Lord Yahweh is coming to my help,
       who dare condemn me?
      They shall all go to pieces like a garment
       devoured by moths.

Reflection:

10   Let anyone who fears Yahweh among you
      listen to the voice of his servant!
     Whoever walks in darkness,
      and has no light shining for him,
     let him trust in the name of Yahweh,
     let him lean on his God.

11   But you, you are all setting light to a fire,
      and fanning embers.
     Then in with you to the flames of your fire,
      to the embers you are lighting.
     So will my hand deal with you
     and you shall lie down in torments.

In the third song, the servant describes his early morning quiet listening during which God teaches him how to respond to the wearied, his unresistant response to those who strike him, and his confidence that God is at hand. In the reflection Isaiah calls those with ears to hear to listen to the voice of the servant and to trust God; but those who fan their own flames will be thrown into the fire.

Fourth Song of the Servant of Yahweh (Isaiah 52:13—53:12)

Song:

13   See, my servant will prosper,
      he shall be lifted up, exalted, rise to great heights!

14   As the crowds were appalled on seeing him
      —so disfigured did he look

that he seemed no longer human—
15 so will the crowds be astonished at him,
and kings stand speechless before him;
for they shall see something never told
and witness something never heard before:

1 'Who could believe what we have heard,
and to whom has the power of Yahweh been revealed?'
2 Like a sapling he grew up in front of us,
like a root in arid ground.
Without beauty, without majesty we saw him,
no looks to attract our eyes;
3 a thing despised and rejected by men,
a man of sorrows and familiar with suffering,
a man to make people screen their faces;
he was despised and we took no account of him.

4 And yet ours were the sufferings he bore,
ours the sorrows he carried.
But we, we thought of him as someone punished,
struck by God, and brought low.
5 Yet he was pierced through for our faults,
crushed for our sins.
On him lies a punishment that brings us peace,
and through his wounds we are healed.

6 We had all gone astray like sheep,
each taking his own way,
and Yahweh burdened him
with the sins of all of us.
7 Harshly dealt with, he bore it humbly,
he never opened his mouth,
like a lamb that is led to the slaughter-house,
like a sheep that is dumb before its shearers
never opening its mouth.

8 By force and by law he was taken;
Would anyone plead his cause?

"Follow Me."

> Yes, he was torn away from the land of the living;
> for our faults struck down in death.
> 9   They gave him a grave with the wicked,
> a tomb with the rich,
> though he had done no wrong
> and there had been no perjury in his mouth."

Reflection:

10   Yahweh has been pleased to crush him with suffering.
If he offers his life in atonement,
he shall see his heirs, he shall have a long life
and through him what Yahweh wishes will be done.

11   His soul's anguish over
he shall see the light and be content.
By his sufferings shall my servant justify many,
taking their faults on himself.

12   Hence I will grant whole hordes for his tribute,
he shall divide the spoil with the mighty,
for surrendering himself to death
and letting himself be taken for a sinner,
while he was bearing the faults of many,
and praying all the time for sinners.

The fourth song presents an astounding turn of events. It begins with God's proclamation: "My servant shall be exalted." The voice of the prophet then describes kings and crowds of people appalled at the sight of the servant, speechless before him. The voice of the people utters our astonishment at the servant's suffering and death, at his humble dignity in suffering, and at the realization that he died because of our faults. In the reflection the prophet sees that this suffering falls within God's will. The song ends with God's affirmation of his servant, the claim that his suffering atones for human sin, and that God's will has been accomplished.

An Interpretation

The four servant songs in context of the earlier Isaiah teaching about the Davidic king provide a portrait for God's Messiah that Jesus consciously chose to live. The fourth servant song in particular provides an account from Jewish Scripture that Jesus may have taken as a foundation for his teaching that he must go to Jerusalem, suffer there at the hands of the leaders, and die there for the redemption of many sinners. Of course, the Jerusalem predictions Jesus made along the way include details that are certainly not in the songs. The resurrection he expected in three days at God's hand goes beyond the songs. Yet Jesus was confident that the way he was traveling accords with God's way of thinking and is the way of the Lord.

If Jesus used these songs as a personal guide, he had certainly come to understand them in a way that was uniquely his own. The fourth song is a far cry from the kind of victory commonly expected for David's anointed son. That God's victory would be brought about through the Messiah's crucifixion and confirmed by his resurrection was not an expectation of Judaism in Mark's time, nor indeed in our own.

Two things are certain. Jesus did not enact these songs by rote. The actions recorded throughout Jesus' ministry belie that claim. He was too open to life around him, responding to the immediate problems and persons who came into his path. The songs provide a guiding light rather than a detailed script to follow. However, we must also note that the tone and general character of his ministry are sounded in these songs. Jesus' early ministry and teaching fit the tenor of the first three songs. The fourth song gives a general pattern descriptive of the way Jesus comported himself before the religious leaders and Pilate. It also provides a powerful interpretation for Jesus' death as bearing our sins, as enacting God's will for our redemption, and providing the vehicle for God's ultimate victory. For this "my servant shall be exalted!"

Bibliography

Betz, Otto. "The Dead Sea Scrolls." In *Interpreter's Dictionary of The Bible Volume 1*, edited by George Arthur Buttrick, 790–802. Nashville: Abingdon, 1962.

Brown, Raymond E. *The Death of the Messiah: From Gethsemane to the Grave*. New York: Doubleday, 1994.

———. *An Introduction to the New Testament*. New York: Doubleday, 1997.

Buttrick, George Arthur, ed. *The Interpreter's Dictionary of the Bible*, 4 vols. Nashville: Abingdon, 1962.

Corbo, Virgilio. *The House of St. Peter at Capharnaum*. Translated by Sylvester Saller. Jerusalem: Franciscan Printing, 1969.

Dahl, Nils Alstrup. "The Crucified Messiah." In *The Crucified Messiah and Other Essays* by Nils Alstrup Dahl, 10–36. Minneapolis: Augsburg, 1974.

Danby, Herbert. *The Mishnah: Translated from the Hebrew with Introduction and Brief Explanatory Notes*. New York: Oxford University Press, 1933.

Flemington, W. F. "Baptism." In *Interpreter's Dictionary of The Bible Volume 1*, edited by George Arthur Buttrick, 348–53. Nashville: Abingdon, 1962.

Gaster, T.H. "Satan." In *Interpreter's Dictionary of The Bible Volume 4*, edited by George Arthur Buttrick, 224–28. Nashville: Abingdon, 1962.

Jeremias, Joachim. *The Eucharistic Words of Jesus*. Translated by Norman Perrin. London: SCM, 1966.

———. *Jerusalem in the Time of Jesus: An Investigation into Economic and Social Conditions during the New Testament Period*. Translated by F.H. and C.H. Cave. Philadelphia: Fortress, 1969.

———. *The Parables of Jesus*. Translated by S.H. Hooke. New York: Charles Scribner, 1972.

Johnson, Luke Timothy. *Brother of Jesus, Friend of God: Studies in the Letter of James*. Grand Rapids, MI: Eerdmans, 2004.

Juel, Donald H. *Messianic Exegesis: Christological Interpretation of the Old Testament in Early Christianity*. Philadelphia: Fortress, 1988.

Knox, J. "Caesar." In *Interpreter's Dictionary of The Bible Volume 1*, edited by George Arthur Buttrick, 478. Nashville: Abingdon, 1962.

Levine, Amy-Jill. *The Misunderstood Jew: The Church and the Scandal of the Jewish Jesus*. New York: HarperCollins, 2006.

Markus, Joel. *The Mystery of the Kingdom of God*. Society of Biblical Literature Dissertation Studies 90. Atlanta: Scholars, 1986.

Bibliography

———. *The Way of the Lord: Christological Exegesis of the Old Testament in the Gospel of Mark*. Louisville, KY: Westminster/John Knox, 1992.

Nestle, Eberhard, et al., eds. *The Greek New Testament*. 27th ed. Deutsche Bibelgesellschaft: Stuttgart, 1933.

Riesner, Rainer. "Jesus, the Primitive Community, and the Essene Quarter of Jerusalem." In *Jesus and the Dead Sea Scrolls*, edited by James H. Charlesworth, 198–234. New York: Doubleday, 1992.

Stinespring, W.F. "Temple, Jerusalem." In *Interpreter's Dictionary of The Bible Volume 4*, edited by George Arthur Buttrick, 534–60. Nashville: Abingdon, 1962.

Vermes, Geza. *Jesus the Jew: A Historian's Reading of the Gospels*. Philadelphia: Fortress, 1973.

Wolf, C.U. "Fishing." In *Interpreter's Dictionary of The Bible Volume 2*, edited by George Arthur Buttrick, 273–74. Nashville: Abingdon, 1962.

Wright, N. T. *The New Testament and the People of God*. Minneapolis: Fortress, 1992.

www.ingramcontent.com/pod-product-compliance
Lightning Source LLC
Chambersburg PA
CBHW051937160426
43198CB00013B/2189